THE
SELECTIVE
ESTATE
AGENT

HOW TO ATTRACT & CONVERT
HIGH VALUE HOMES

SAM ASHDOWN

R3THINK PRESS

First published in Great Britain in 2020 by Rethink Press
(www.rethinkpress.com)

Printed and bound by CPI Group (UK) Ltd, Croydon, CR0 4YY

Praise

'A highly insightful and hugely useful
marketing strategy resource for ambitious,
growth minded estate agents. This book covers
a wide range of ideas, concepts and practical
techniques to help establish your agency as a
local market leader. A recommended read for
those independent property professionals, and
their teams, who seek market differentiation
and look to implement operational excellence.'
   – **Oliver Gleave**, Loop Software and Jupix
      founder

'I have built several brands online and many
points of the book by Sam I have myself used
in the past, so I can say they work. Sam makes
the process of achieving simple in her book,
though rightly does not paint a picture that
it is easy or that you'll be rewarded without
efforts – by working the process Sam has set
you stand a better chance of success. I'm a
believer in the power of content marketing and

positioning yourself as a go to person/name for information, which I am pleased Sam also highlights the importance of.'

    – **Christopher Walkey**, Founder of Estate Agent Networking

'This book is perfect for independent agents wanting to set themselves apart from the competition with high value homes. Sam's views on marketing are refreshingly different, but more importantly they work! Sam gets deep into the mind of the client and tailors her approach to suit – a great must-have book for every independent estate agent.'

    – **John Paul**, CEO The Castledene Group

'Great book! A must read for estate agent directors wanting to build the "go to" agency for high end homes in their area. Sam's experience as a consultant and estate agency director shines through with actionable tactics and an implementable playbook.'

    – **Rajeev Nayyar**, Managing Director, Fixflo

'In all my 25+ years in the Estate Agency industry, I have never come across a Guide or Book that helps Estate Agents focus their marketing & tactics to attract the upper quartile of the property market. What Sam Ashdown has done with her Direct Mail,

Content ideas and Sales funnels is a step by step guide that works to attract upmarket house sellers for your agency – and it has already been proved to work for Sam's Estate Agency, by making her the #1 agent for 'posh' houses in Lakes within 30 months.'
> – **Christopher Watkin**, Content Expert to the Property Industry

'Whether you are thinking of opening an estate agency, or like me been in the business for 35 years and think you've seen it all, then prepare yourself for the most informative and innovative book on the industry I have *ever* read. A chance to review what works, to bin what doesn't and to try what really might. Sam is that unusual being – a business consultant who has followed her own advice! In this book, she answers the questions that no one else does and provides inspiration based on real strategy that will encourage you to new successes.'
> – **Henry Pryor**, 'The BBC's Favourite Property Expert'

'What an amazing book for any agent that wants to just ooze quality and stand out, secure the highest value and top listings in the market and retain the best clients at a time when instructions are thin on the ground and competition is fierce…It's a truly awesome

read, I would recommend this book to any estate agents starting out on a mission to be the BEST and to secure the top clients.'
   – **Sally Lawson**, Founder of Agent
      Rainmaker

Contents

*To my mum, Judy. You were right –
every cloud does have a silver lining.*

Introduction

Why should you listen to me?

A good question. After all, I've only been an estate agent since 2017.

Over a noisy family Christmas dinner back in 2016, my son-in-law Phil (Jones) turned to me and said something that was to have bigger consequences than either of us could have ever guessed. He said: 'Let's open an estate agency'.

At first, I resisted, strongly. I had a pile of excuses: not enough time, too much competition, not enough money, too much stress. Eventually, though, he won. And a few weeks later, on 1st April 2017, Phil left his previous employment and AshdownJones became a reality.

We had no website, no Rightmove and no credibility. I had been teaching independent estate agents my unique marketing systems for many years, and extolling the benefits of quality over quantity, and now here I was, putting my money where my mouth was. And it was pretty damn scary. Because if it didn't work, my coaching clients would lose faith in me, and I would lose all authority in the industry. After all, who's going to hire an estate agency coach who can't run their own agency?

On top of this, we were risking so much personally, sinking our hard-earned savings into a brand-new venture in a completely new area, when neither of us had any proof we could even sell a house. There was so much at stake, we just couldn't fail.

We launched from my dining room. Just Phil, me and a couple of laptops. But the difference between us and other cold-start agencies is that we knew what we needed to do to get the phone ringing. Rarely does a marketing coach open an agency – in fact, I've never heard of another that has – even though many estate agents have done the opposite and begun offering coaching. By starting as a marketing coach, I'd be able to put into practice everything I'd been teaching and refining for the last fifteen years, starting with our launch plan, using the PROFIT Pyramid™. On day one of our launch, we sent our first batch of direct mail (Cornerstone #1), and within six months we'd listed £170,000 in fees, including our first house (the first of many) over £1 million.

In our first thirteen months, we passed the milestone of reaching £500,000 in listed and sold fees.

Within two years, we were listing and selling more homes over £500,000 than any of the other fifty-seven agents in the Lakes. In 2018, we sold two of seven £1 million houses sold that year. At the time of writing, we now have thirteen homes listed at £1 million and above.

Why I wrote this book

Way back in 2004, while Mark Zuckerberg was still at university and the UK was heading for the biggest property bubble in history, I launched HomeTruths – an advisory service for people selling their homes. Over the years, HomeTruths became synonymous with high value homes, our consultants commanding several thousands of pounds in consultancy fees and in turn getting unprecedented results using my carefully crafted marketing methodology. We were selling houses no one else could, at an average of 92% of asking price, sometimes after many years of marketing. And we weren't estate agents.

Eventually, independent estate agents started to notice what we were doing; they asked me to help them, first with their stale stock and then, later, with their agency marketing. By 2012, I'd launched my estate agency coaching practice – Sam Ashdown Coaching – and was working directly with estate agents, helping them create and implement marketing strategies. It was the aftermath of the biggest crash we had ever experienced in the property industry, and the agencies that had survived, battered and bruised, were understandably nervous about spending money on marketing – or anything, for that matter, that might not bring in a return on their investment.

My marketing strategies and tactics had to be foolproof, easy to follow and yet difficult for their competitors to copy. The challenge was not an easy one, but I put my heart and soul into rising to it for them. Some of my clients had become my friends – and in fact, some of my agency friends had become my clients. I just couldn't let them down. What I taught them had to work. They each had so much on the line. And by association, so did I.

I tried as many different marketing techniques as possible myself and gave them to my clients to test. Some were big new ideas, others just simple tweaks. I was obsessed with finding cost-effective tactics that would significantly boost my clients' enquiries and instructions and increase their bottom line. Over the years, I've tried every different type of marketing tactic you can think of to help independent agencies get their phones ringing with quality new instructions. Some failed spectacularly. Others seemed like no-brainer brilliant ideas, but they, too, didn't work. Eventually, just three marketing strategies began to emerge as working better than anything else I was teaching. Wary of advising my clients to put all their marketing efforts and spend into any one avenue, I felt these three marketing strategies – what become known as our 'cornerstones' – were robust enough to form the foundation of any independent agency's growth plans, even in the future when the fast-paced marketing world was to change significantly.

I have rigorously tested these three marketing cornerstones that now make up the PROFIT Pyramid™ with over 200 agencies, over several years, and they have consistently and dependably produced great results for every single agency, including ours. But more on that coming up.

In this book, I'll share in detail my PROFIT Pyramid™, show you some of the behind-the-scenes of our agency, and give you the tools and resources you need to implement the PROFIT Pyramid™ in your agency. By the time you've finished this book, you'll be ready and able to take your agency to a whole new level of profitability in the fastest, most cost-effective way possible.

This book is simple and straightforward but packed with strategies and tips I guarantee you won't find anywhere else. Use it as a guide to help you achieve your business goals and create a lifestyle agency, whether you're a start-up, early-growth or established agency.

This leads me on to the next question you may be asking...

Who is this book for?

Let's start by talking about who this book is not for: corporate agencies and non-executive employees (unless they're thinking of jumping ship and starting their own agency) won't get much out of this book if they can't action the daringly bold strategies I outline. Also, if you're an agency owner looking to grow by a high-volume, low-fees strategy, this book is not for you. That, my friend, is a Red Ocean strategy, and I only share Blue Ocean strategies in this book. If you've never heard of the terms 'Red Ocean' and 'Blue Ocean', here's a brief explanation:

Red Ocean companies compete in a crowded space, trying to grab their piece of an ever-decreasing pie. The market becomes commoditised and only the best-funded companies survive.

Blue Ocean companies don't need to compete on price because they have created true differentiation, and although imitators will always appear, the Blue Ocean company is way ahead and constantly innovating to stay there.[1]

I wrote this book for you if you are an ambitious independent estate agent who wants to grow your agency

---

1   Chan Kim, W and Maugborne, R (2015) *Blue Ocean Strategy*. Harvard Business School Press

without fuss or stress and create a beautiful lifestyle business you can sell in the future, if you want to.

I know that right now you're probably juggling work and home life, and wondering where you're going to somehow find the extra hours you think you'll need to make these strategies work for you. But I can promise you that once you learn the secrets of my High Value Homes Attraction and Conversion Strategy, you'll realise you can generate more revenue and create more profit, *and* do it in less time than you're currently spending on marketing techniques that are probably not working for you. You can also discard that business model that is leaving you exhausted and devoid of inspiration. All that is going to change when you read and implement the ideas in this book.

How do I know? Because I've coached thousands of independent agents just like you in redesigning their businesses to fit them, instead of them always trying to fit their lifestyles around their business needs. When you take control of your business, something wonderful happens: you fall in love with it all over again. Remember that spark of excitement and wonderment that you started your agency with in the first place? Maybe you feel you've lost it. But it's still there, I promise you. It's just temporarily buried under a mountain of paperwork and AML forms. I'm going to show you how to find it, dust it off and polish it to a brilliant shine for all the world to see.

Your problem

Phil and I speak to independent agents like you every single day. That's what we do. We both love to hear what's working for them right now and what their biggest marketing challenges are. And what we've discovered is that most agents have a serious problem: they are wasting money on marketing that doesn't work. And these are not small amounts.

I recently spoke to an agent in Colchester who was spending £80,000 a year on advertising and marketing. And that didn't even include her portal spend. She was paying for a mixture of PR, newspaper and magazine advertising, canvassing, and a ton of fancy software they weren't even using. This kind of spend just isn't sustainable. As a comparison, we spend less than £3,000 a year in order to generate a turnover that is far higher than this agency's.

Stop wasting money on marketing that isn't working

You have been misled, often misadvised and bamboozled, and on occasion you may even have been ripped off. How are you supposed to know what actually works? How can you identify the marketing activities that work, and ditch the ones that don't? After all, everyone is trying to sell you the silver bullet they think you need.

Let's have a look at the kinds of services some independent agents I know are subscribed to:

- Content marketing – £300 a month
- Social media management – £250 a month
- Facebook ad management – £500 a month plus ad spend
- Search engine optimisation (SEO) – £400 a month
- Google AdWords – £500 a month plus ad spend
- Market research – £300 a month
- Rightmove Optimise – £1,500 a month

The total possible spend on this 'lead generation' is £45,000+ per year – which might be palatable if it worked. But it doesn't. Say yes to everything and financial ruin lies just ahead.

So, what's going to work for you? What do you need to do to meet your goals this year and next? If you don't find out what marketing actions work in the real world, bad things will happen to you. If you never have enough quality valuations in your diary, then your staff will leave. Staff don't like to be in an agency that is struggling for business and in which the boss seems perpetually worried. The best ones will simply leave for a more successful competitor – or perhaps even become one, knowing your biggest weakness lies in your inability to generate a consistent supply of quality leads.

When you're scrapping around for barely profitable instructions, every day becomes a fight. Having consulted to many agents in this position, I know that when they go into the office they're already anxious about the day ahead, feeling constantly overdrawn – physically and financially – and heavily burdened by their problems.

There is another way. You can discover what marketing works for your agency to bring in those instructions that make you smile on those homes you'd love to put your board outside. When your diary is full with the best, most profitable and enjoyable valuations, your team will love you – because who doesn't want to work in a successful agency? The money will start to come in more consistently, and with a healthy bank balance you can focus on taking your agency to the next level, to become a brand you can be proud of, and one that creates impact and legacy for the future.

If all that's standing between you and this kind of success for your agency, we can help you, just like we've helped thousands and thousands of independent agency owners just like you.

If you'd like to know more about how we could help you install and implement the PROFIT Pyramid™ in your agency, go to http://bit.ly/bookacallwithsam and book a call with me.

My solution

The Selective Estate Agent is a how-to book that helps independent estate agents grow their businesses and add additional revenue without losing their bread-and-butter income.

In this book, I demonstrate how you can create and apply a High Value Homes Strategy in your agency to build your brand image, gain new profitable clients and generate a new profit stream. And the good news is that you're hearing it straight from the horse's mouth – me. Not only are we using these techniques and practices every single day in our agency, AshdownJones, but I also coach independent agencies on modelling our processes so they can enjoy the same success we do.

Many independent estate agencies are struggling right now, squeezed on fees by the onlines on one side and the mighty corporates on the other. But I'm going to show you that the main reason independent agents are not as profitable as they could be is because they are pursuing the wrong market, in the wrong way. They are looking for profit where very little exists, and in a pool where the big corporates and the onlines are already fishing. I'll show you how to take your little fishing rod to a pool where there is hardly any competition, where the clients will value and appreciate you, and where the real profit is to be found.

This book will show you more than just a few marketing tactics. I'm going to show you how to plan for profitable success by targeting, attracting and selling the best high value homes in your area so that you get the best financial return on your investment. And not only is it probably more straightforward than you think, it's a strategy you can begin implementing today – without sacrificing any of your current bread-and-butter income.

Because here's my vision for your business. It's an agency that fits around you – not the other way around. You have about four or five employees, and with that you're able to attract, list and sell the very best homes in your area. You're creating beautiful marketing that you and your team can be proud of, and that gets your agency noticed for all the right reasons. And instead of working with lots of low-paying, high-maintenance clients who are never going to 'get' your value, you work with only those great clients who love everything you do and who tell their friends about you.

Perhaps when you first launched your agency you had every intention of setting up your business in this way. But maybe you got yourself into a rut of doing the same as every other agent, stuck on a revenue roller coaster. I want to share with you our system that will enable you to build the agency of your dreams – the one you always wanted to own.

Join me in the pages to follow, where I'm going to show you how to attract the best clients, list the best homes and sell at the best fees.

ONE

Your High Value Homes Strategy

How we use a High Value Homes Strategy

When we launched our estate agency in 2017, we faced a challenge many start-up agencies face: a great idea, but no proven track record of sales. How were we going to attract the profitable instructions if we had never sold a house? It was a chicken-and-egg problem we were determined to solve. And we did. In this book, I'll share with you the exact steps we took to grow our agency to where it is today, by adopting the very same principles I'm teaching to you. There is nothing you will read in this book that we have not tried and tested ourselves. If we have tried something and it didn't work, I have not included it here. You're only learning our successful tactics. In short, we've put in the hard work and wasted marketing spend, so you don't have to.

I want to:

- Show you that you're closer than you think to owning a successful, profitable agency without stress or overwhelm
- Help you focus on what you genuinely want your agency to do for you
- Inspire you to create the agency you always dreamed you'd own
- Share my experiences of running a successful estate agency only selling high value homes
- Show you some simple steps you can take to create powerful and profitable results for your agency
- Give you the confidence you may be lacking to target and convert the homes you'd love to sell

This strategy will work for you, too. All you need to do is to follow the steps in this book, and create and implement your 90-Day Implementation Plan, available as a download at www.samashdown.co.uk /theselectiveagentbook, and I promise you will almost immediately start seeing the same successes we've enjoyed. Our achievement is not a one-off; hundreds of independent agents all over the country – and as far afield as South Africa, North America and Iceland – have also seen successes like ours. You'll hear from some of them in the coming pages; but for now, let's dive into...

The financial case for your High Value Homes Strategy

What does your stock ratio look like at the moment? If it's like that of most other independent agents in the UK, you have around forty houses on the market, with a ratio that looks something like this:

1 over £1 million

3 at £500,000–£1 million

17 between £250,000 and £500,000

20 under £250,000

Total value of listed fees at 1%: around £140,000 (making some assumptions on the actual asking prices)

Now imagine you could attract just ten new, high value homes, in addition to your current stock, and at a higher fee. Say, 1.5% and an average asking price of £700,000. That will add another £105,000 in fees to your top line. That's a 75% increase, for a 25% increase in stock – for just ten new instructions.

The difference? These are high value homes. And they're listed at high value fees. But how do you attract and win high value homes, without sacrificing any of your core revenue? After all, your bread-and-butter sales pay for your office and payroll, so you need to make sure you still get the two-bed terraces and three-bed semis. I understand. But here's where the fun starts, because these new homes are *additional* fees. And the best news is that you can attract, win and sell these homes with no additional resources.

Getting more profit out of fewer sales is what this strategy is all about. It's time to stop taking on low value, unappreciative clients who are not prepared to pay the fees you're worth. It's time to take control of your time, your finances and your future. It's time to wise up, level up and play a bigger game.

Don't you want more?

If you do what other agents are doing, you'll get what other agents get. Don't you want more?

If I told you that you have all you need, right here in this book, to change your life, and all you have to do is look at your business in a different way, would you do it? Because no matter where you are in your business right now, the thinking that got you here won't get you where you want to go next. The strategy and tactics you deployed to get you to the pre-launch phase of your agency won't get you beyond that tricky first year. The thinking that helped you beat the odds and survive to year two with your fledgling agency is not the same thinking that will get you to that five-year milestone. And when you do get to celebrate your half-decade in business, you'll find that securing a consistent five-figure personal income every month needs new thinking once again. To take your agency to the next level – whatever that next level means to you – requires a significant mindset shift at each step.

It could be that you're just starting out and want to launch your brand-new agency with maximum impact. Or perhaps you want to grow slowly and steadily, adding just 10% to your top line each year. Maybe you're dedicated to maximum growth and you have set your sights on doubling or trebling your revenue over the next five years. It could be that you want to grow your business by creating a multi-branch network. Or perhaps what's important to you right now is creating a robust exit strategy that will leave you with a financially secure retirement.

Your 'next level' of business success is unique to you, and it's what fuels your *why*. Your *why* is what gets you out of bed in the morning, ready to face whatever a day in the life of an estate agency owner will throw at you. It's what helps you navigate obstacles, deal with conflict, manage chaotic cash-flow and spin more plates than a circus performer. And to do it (most of the time) with a smile on your face. It's all because of your *why*. Your *why* is personal to you, whether it's your family, your financial future or your need to prove yourself professionally. Perhaps you've always wanted an Aston Martin, a holiday home in the sun, or to take a year off and go travelling.

Your *why* is what keeps you going. But there's a catch. I'm here to tell you that your *why* on its own won't get you there. It'll help to keep you motivated and determined, but if you don't have the right mindset your *why* will not succeed in its quest to get you what you dearly wish for. Your mindset is the most powerful tool you have in your business. And I'm going to show you how to use it to transform your agency, reach your highest goals and live the lifestyle you've always dreamed of.

What's stopping you from winning the fees you deserve?

Is your average fee closer to £10,000 or £2,000? At AshdownJones, our current average fee is over £11,000. It's been much higher in the past, and it may dip lower if we have a run of properties at asking prices of less than £600,000. Even if you've never charged a fee this high before, when you follow the system set out in this book you'll be able to charge the fee you deserve, whether that's 1.5%, 1.75% or even over 2%.

Last year, I started working with a lovely client I'll call Joe. Joe had just bought an agency franchise for his area in Lancashire, and he followed their marketing guide to the letter. But it didn't work. All he ended up with was a giant hole in his bank account from failed

Google Ads, and sore knuckles from posting leaflets through thousands of letterboxes. On our first call, he told me he knew he had to do something drastic or he was going to go out of business – and we were talking not months, but weeks. He was literally running out of money and even considering getting a different job.

Joe took the plunge of investing in my coaching programme and discovered the PROFIT Pyramid™, which he loved. He followed each step faithfully and methodically, with trust and motivation, and to his astonishment (but not mine) he was soon getting invited out to the premium properties on his patch. Although he started at just a 1% fee, he was soon able to increase it 1.25%, and by the time you read this he should now be charging 1.5%. And this in an area where the average agency fees are 0.75% or even less. What I find exciting is that Joe's three-year revenue goal is now his *one-year* revenue goal. He's absolutely flying, and he's loving the journey.

Why aren't you growing your business as fast as Joe is?

I know how frustrating it can be to try to build your business feeling like you've got one hand (or both) tied behind your back. I know because I used to be you. I know what it's like to struggle in my business. I know what it's like to have no clients. I know what it's like to have no confidence in my fees, afraid that if you charge more no one will pay it. And I know what it's like to lie awake at night wondering where my next client will come from, listening to my voice of doubt saying, 'Why don't you just give it up and get a proper job?'

I just happened to discover and then develop the best system in the world for building an independent estate agency that is profitable, sustainable and growing. My system allows independent agents like us to experience the freedom of attracting the clients we want at the fees we deserve. It's the same system that's allowed my clients to double their instructions and triple their profit, time and time again. Even brand-new agents like Joe can turn their long-term income goals into their short-term income goals – all while getting amazing results for their clients and helping them to move on with their lives.

After working with thousands of independent agents from all over the UK, I have discovered the obstacles that will sabotage an agent's efforts to attract great clients and why it's not their fault they struggle to get through the right doors. The real problem is that they have been given bad advice that wasted their time with a bunch of boring, outdated and exhausting marketing strategies that just don't work; strategies that steal their time, drain their bank account and leave them with absolutely nothing to show for it.

The answers have changed

According to an apocryphal anecdote, Albert Einstein, having just given an exam paper to his Princeton students, was asked by his teaching assistant, 'Dr Einstein, wasn't that exam the same one you gave to this same class of physics students last year?'

Einstein nodded. 'Yes, it was the same exam.'

'But Dr Einstein,' protested the assistant, 'how could you give the same exam to the same class two years in a row?'

Einstein thought for a moment and then said, 'Well, the answers have changed.'

So it is in estate agency marketing. The questions are the same. Common questions in estate agency marketing include: How can we get the phone to ring? How do I get through more doors? How can I increase my fees? But the answers have changed and are constantly continuing to change. The quest for profit – and, in some cases, simply for survival – calls for a continuous, ongoing process of strategic and tactical marketing activities.

Stop what's not working, now

If you don't, you'll waste tons of time and money on useless marketing, expecting your ideal clients will somehow find you and then hoping that, somehow, eventually they might invite you to give them a market appraisal. This is 'spray-and-pray' marketing, and it doesn't work.

You spend hours each week trying to make it work, using up your precious energy and money, and never seeing an improvement in your bank balance. This is not what I want for you, and I know it's not what you want for yourself. And this is why it's not your fault if you're struggling to get invited out to the best properties. You've simply been given bad advice.

When you have a system for attracting the best clients at the highest fees, the money comes in very quickly. You don't have to push out a bunch of leaflets and pray you'll get a load of phone calls. When you learn and implement this system, you'll know exactly where your next instruction is coming from.

Packaging signifies quality

Take the humble paperclip; how much would you pay for one? Five pence? Less? If you needed to buy paperclips, you may turn to Staples or Viking, where you can buy 100 paperclips for 71p. That's 0.07p per paperclip.

Have you looked on the Tiffany website recently? It features a beautiful paperclip, designed for use as a bookmark. It's 2.5 inches long and made of sterling silver, and it's £155. You read that right. There are people in this world who are happy to pay £155 for a paperclip. But not from Staples. They want the whole package: the beautiful blue box, the silky ribbon and, most importantly, the Tiffany name embossed on it. Because that's where the value lies to someone who appreciates Tiffany.

Just as there are buyers for a £155 paperclip, there are also homeowners who would be prepared to pay 5% for a company to sell their house, if only an agent would offer the right service to them. The highest fee I know of in the UK is 3%, but the agents charging at this level are few and far between. After all, no one would pay more to sell their house, right?

Wrong. The only limit on fees is in the mindset of the estate agent. Yes, there are homeowners who are fee sensitive, just as there are people who would never pay more than a few pence for a paperclip. But if everyone bought on price, we'd all be driving Dacia cars and going camping instead of abroad for our family holidays, and the Fat Duck at Bray would have closed down years ago. No one is fully servicing the top of the property market in the UK. But you can. I'm not suggesting you charge 3%, or even 2%, if that feels a step too far; but I am going to recommend that your pricing strategy should be at least a quarter of a percent above that of your nearest competitor. In doing so, you're positioning yourself well away from their lesser service and experience. You can't be the cheapest *and* the best. You have to choose, so choose to be the best.

Tangible property marketing beats promised service levels

Imagine you're in a valuation appointment, promising your potential vendor the very best service. Don't you think they've heard those promises from the other two agents they've interviewed? They've almost certainly said exactly the same things you have: how hard they will work and how they are absolutely sure they will be able to sell their home for the price they want, in the timeframe they need. Promises are cheap, but your bespoke brochures are proof you carry out your promises.

Our beautiful brochures at AshdownJones are literally worth more than their weight in gold. One of our brochures weighs around 100 grams, and 100 grams of gold is worth roughly £3,000. How much could yours be worth? Let's work it out:

Let's say you take on a high value home with a £10,000 fee (say, £666,000 at 1.5%), and you get to work creating the best marketing package you have ever produced. You style the home so it looks amazing, create a bespoke for-sale board, commission a specialist lifestyle photographer and have some twilight drone images taken. You get a professional copywriter to interview your vendor and produce poetic copy describing the home in an aspirational way. Then you work with a talented designer to create a beautiful bespoke brochure that befits the home and wows your client. Congratulations, you've taken the first big step to implementing a High Value Homes Strategy. Here's what you need to do next:

With your brochure in hand, you can approach other high value homes and show them what you can do for them. Let's say you generate three valuation appointments and win two instructions (66% conversion). For these new high value instructions, you repeat your marketing creation process, with the result that you now have three brochure examples and £30,000 in listed.

If you can take on a new high value home each month using this formula, you'll add £120,000 in fees to your top line. Even if only ten of these homes sell within a year, you'll generate £100,000 in extra revenue. How does that sound? How would that change your business finances, and your lifestyle?

In AshdownJones' first thirteen months, we listed fifty homes, with a fee value of £500,000. From a cold-start launch, and using only our bespoke property marketing as a differentiator, we were able to successfully build a reputation for selling the best homes in our area, and this reputation grew with every home we listed with our unique marketing. Our High Value Homes Strategy created a momentum of its own, making each new enquiry more valuable and each valuation appointment easier to convert to instruction.

First through HomeTruths, and then with Sam Ashdown Coaching, I have over fifteen years of experience in the unique and exclusive property marketing arena. I've worked with thousands of homeowners and independent estate agency owners, and hundreds of industry suppliers, including photographers, home stylists, property stagers, designers, copywriters and printers. In short, I believe I know more about exactly what property marketing appeals to the owners of high value homes than anyone else in the industry.

How a High Value Homes Strategy will transform your agency

It will give you massive confidence

Having the best marketing will give you supreme confidence with high value clients. When you show your beautiful brochures and bespoke sale boards to a homeowner, you'll find yourself doing so with pride and conviction that this will be the very best property marketing they've ever seen.

You'll create excitement

You'll enjoy watching your clients' wonder and admiration as they peruse your brochures with pleasure, imagining their home looking stunning and showcased in one of your fabulous brochures.

Your offer will be utterly compelling

The best vendors will find your marketing irresistible; the clients you want to attract – those who 'get' your brochures – will find them impossible to resist. They will realise that not only do they need (and want) these brochures created for their own home but also that no other agent can create them. Therefore, if they want a beautiful, bespoke brochure, they need to instruct you to sell their home.

It will give you an invaluable competitive edge

Unless they're reading this book or they've been a client of mine, your competitors have no idea how to create this level of bespoke marketing. They lack the know-how and the motivation to go to the effort and expense of creating brochures of the same quality. This is your competitive advantage, and you'll feel the benefit of it when you start implementing this strategy.

You need a high growth strategy

Don't confuse the term 'strategy' with its sister, 'tactic'. A strategy is simply a general term for a plan; in this context, it's a plan of action designed to help you achieve your goals. It's how you're going to get there, without getting into the weeds – the 'tactics', which are all the specific actions you'll need to take.

For example, your growth strategy could be to target only high value homes, whereas the tactics you plan to use might include direct mail and Facebook advertising. Now you know the difference between a strategy and a tactic, let's look at the strategy we use at AshdownJones to help us achieve our goal of being the number-one agent in our area for high value homes.

Your strategy controls everything that you do in your business. It even controls the culture of your business – and therefore how your team perform. Where you direct your focus dictates your results. We knew when we first launched AshdownJones that our strategy had to be robust in its planning and bold in its execution. Because we decided to relentlessly pursue a strategy of selectivity, everything we do is about attracting, converting and selling only unique homes in our area.

Being selective means you don't take on every house that you go to see. Turning down business is hard, but it has been the secret to our success. Because we only take on unique homes (and these tend to be the high value homes in our area, anyway), we attract more of the same. We get asked to list unique homes *because we only list unique homes*. We're considered specialists and expert in selling high value homes. It's a virtuous cycle.

I know how tempted you are to take on any property you are offered. That grotty flat over the chippy; the house with the smelly dogs; the client that is never, ever satisfied, even though he's paying half a percent less than anyone else. But it makes sense to eliminate the weeds, which are taking time, energy and money away from your best business, and then identify your VIPs and heap upon them the love, care and attention that they deserve.

Although I'm sure you love all your clients dearly, (perhaps some more than others), you may notice that a disproportionate number of your lower-level clients are taking up all your time and energy (and that of your team). This is time and energy you should be spending on your best clients – those who are paying you the most. After all, your time and energy are finite, and there may be occasions when you drop the ball, miss an important deadline, fail to follow up or forget a call because you are spreading yourself too thinly.

To remedy this situation, stop taking on those low-level clients – the ones whose houses don't excite you. Instead, actively seek instructions from innovative, inspirational clients who get you, and put your fees up – a lot. By doing this, you'll have plenty of time to spend on the clients for whom you can make the biggest difference, and who motivate and stimulate you whenever you work with them.

Being selective is a mindset, and one that is often hard one to adopt. You will doubt yourself. After all, a low fee is still a fee; how will your business survive without those small sales? Here's the problem with this way of thinking: each £2,000 fee could cost you a £20,000 fee. If our listings were full of terraces and flats, then the next person looking for an agent for their £2 million home isn't going to give us a thought. Nobody wants their house to be the most expensive in an agent's portfolio; it would make them lack confidence in your ability to sell their home.

Selectivity is another word for profitability

One of my clients called me recently from outside a valuation appointment. 'I don't think I really want this one,' she told me. She explained that the homeowner had been a bit difficult when arranging the appointment, and that it had already been on the market with another agent for several months. It was a nice property, recently marketed at £350,000.

'What should I do?' she asked.

'Over-fee and under-value' I told her.

So, she did. She went in at 1.8% and told the vendor the price needed to come down to £300,000.

Guess what happened? Yep, she got it – but at an asking price she could sell for and a fee that would make a needy vendor worth the extra time and effort.

What would it mean to you to be selective? You would have more time for the same profit – or even more – than you currently show. Your team would be more relaxed, not running around like headless chickens. You would be proud of your register, which would be full of lovely properties that showcase your brand. Your marketing would be educative and created to attract leads, not in the me-me-me mass leafleting style. And the bottom line is that with a sustainable model like this, you can grow your agency without being stressed and overwhelmed.

TWO

Your High Value Homes Delivery

Deliver a differentiated service using bespoke property marketing

It's time to turn our attention to the elements of bespoke property marketing you'll need to create to wow your prospects and surprise and delight your clients.

In this chapter, I'll go into detail on each and every part of the bespoke property marketing you'll need to offer, how to create it, and why property technology won't help you attract and convert the clients you want.

How do you attract the very best clients? Simple: with the very best marketing materials.

When you think of prestige property marketing, which agents come to mind? Fifteen years ago, Savills, Knight

Frank and Fine & Country were agents at the cutting edge of luxury property marketing, leading the way. Now, the property marketing landscape has changed. What was cutting edge is now the new normal. What was innovative is now standard.

To truly stand out to the homeowners you want to attract, you need to take your property marketing to a whole new level.

You can't charge top fees and then deliver only a mediocre service. Owners of large, luxury homes expect a sophisticated marketing service. Professional photography is no longer enough; you need lifestyle images of styled homes.

Unique and exclusive homes need unique and exclusive marketing. Offer this, and you, too, can attract the homes you want.

What is bespoke property marketing?

These are the ten elements of bespoke property marketing that we offer in our agency:

1. Lifestyle photography

2. Drone photography

3. Twilight imagery

4. Local and landscape photography

5. Professional copywriting

6. Homeowner interviews

7. Home styling

8. Individual property branding

9. Printed magazine-style brochures, with specialist print finishes and formats

10. Bespoke for-sale boards

To my knowledge, no other agent offers all ten. This means you have a golden opportunity to create a huge impact in your area, but you'll have to be quick: your biggest competitor could be reading this book right now!

Photography

Photography is the most important element of your bespoke property marketing, where you can most effectively demonstrate differentiation. If you are determined to attract the highest-quality homes and the most discerning clients, while competing with the best premium agencies in your area, you'll need to get your photography absolutely right, every time.

At AshdownJones, we offer four types of photography:

1. Lifestyle photography

2. Drone photography

3. Twilight imagery

4. Local and landscape photography

We find that by creating attractive imagery of the home and its surroundings, we can not only showcase the home more effectively but we also capture the hearts and the confidence of our clients, who love to see their home portrayed so beautifully in our images.

Lifestyle photography

You may have heard the term 'lifestyle photography', but what is it, and why do you need it to promote your high value homes?

Lifestyle photography for properties is when your photographer captures more than the bricks and mortar, and instead shows the lifestyle a buyer can expect to attain if they buy the house. These images help someone build an emotional connection to the house and imagine themselves living there. Lifestyle photography is the kind you see in a quality home magazine: it might be a crackling fire, champagne and glasses on a balcony, or a bubble bath lit by candles.

At AshdownJones, we only sell unique homes, and many of the high value homes in your area will also be one-offs. Showing the house using the same kind of photographs you use for a three-bed semi will do these special homes a disservice. Your new, high value clients will feel pride and delight when you show you've fully understood the real worth of their home and appreciated the lifestyle it offers. By doing so, you elevate not only the home you're marketing, and your estate agency brand by association; you're also elevating the relationship you have with your clients, deepening trust and building loyalty.

Drone photography

While many property photographers now offer drone photography as well as a standard professional imagery, and can offer both in one visit, I suggest you consider keeping these two services separate so as not to put all your eggs in one basket. Our drone photographer often visits twice, once during daylight hours and again at twilight. At some times of the year, and in fine weather, you may be able to schedule these two types of photoshoots back-to-back so the drone photographer just has to wait for it to get a bit darker. But in summertime, when twilight shoots can be as late as 11pm, this may not be feasible. Our Client Services team always attends a twilight shoot so they can make sure we get the exact image we need for the brochure and Rightmove. Standing with the drone photographer and watching their screen while they take the shot can be invaluable, in case they've missed something important. We find that clients often like to be present, too, and enjoy seeing their home from the air.

Twilight imagery

Twilight, or 'dusk', photography usually captures the exterior of the house, shortly after the sun has disappeared or just as it's doing so. This kind of photography shows off outside features like concealed lighting, pagodas strung with fairy lights and fire pits. At the same time, with all the lights in the house lit, twilight photography can make even the most uninspiring façade look attractive, warm and welcoming. A sunset sky as a backdrop is an added bonus, often captured rather by luck than planning, but it can elevate the shot even further to something magical.

We find that by using a twilight photograph as the main image on the portals we can maximise clicks and views of that property online. Because daytime shots are still the norm, twilight images stand out so much more when buyers are looking for a property. In 100 listings on Rightmove, there may be only one or two twilight shots, so make sure these are yours. Not only does this showcase your client's property, it also showcases your agency as one that creates inspirational, stand-out images.

Twilight images are usually taken in the period just after the sun has set, so there is still some light left in the sky. Too dark a sky will render the house invisible; but if the sky is still light, the interior and exterior lighting won't show enough. It's tricky to get the balance right between the two, but once you do the result is a magical image buyers and sellers alike will love.

Local and landscape photography

Sellers love to tell you what local sights and amenities are within a short walk or drive of their home. Buyers, too, want to see what surrounds their potential new home and how they will enjoy the environs in residence. Having beautiful images of local walks, landmarks and scenery will bring the brochure to life, attract buyers and please your clients. Ask your photographer if they already have some local images; you may find a landscape photographer has a library of local images you can purchase. If not, ask them to go to the shoot early and find some local features to photograph. You may also be able to find some stock images on one of the standard stock photography sites that you can use, but remember that your competitors also have access to these, so they won't be unique to you. Better to create your own library, over time, of all the local landmarks in your area. That way, you know you'll always have an image for a brochure that you'll never see used anywhere else.

Photo editing

The fee you agree with your photographers should include all editing. However, I'm a big believer of getting the shot right 'in camera', so your photographers don't have to spend hours in editing that they aren't being directly paid for. Removing a washing line instead of saying, 'You can just take that out in Photoshop, can't you?' will keep your photographer friendly, onside and happy to take on photoshoots for you.

Blue skies – Many agents now feature properties with blue skies instead of dull grey backdrops, but they can look very fake. It's much better to arrange your photoshoot when there is a little blue in the sky that can be enhanced, instead of expecting your photographer to try to laboriously cut out the original white sky, carefully cutting around trees and power lines, and then put in an entirely new sky.

Twilight skies – The same goes for twilight. Yes, there are plenty of companies that can convert your daytime image to a twilight image, but, firstly, it will never look as good as an actual twilight image, and, secondly, if you can do it, so can your competitors. It's easy for them to use tech to try to improve on their own property marketing, but if you're intent on getting an original twilight image with sunset backdrop, theirs just won't match up.

Taking out unsightly elements – It's OK to ask your photographer to edit out an object that's temporary, like a skip or an outside bin. But you can't take out permanent features, like power lines, antennas or telegraph poles.

Property styling

Over the last fifteen years, I've helped style over 1,000 homes to help them look appealing and attractive for photography and viewings. I've also been lucky enough to work with some of the best property stylists, home stagers and photographers in the country; and in doing so, I've picked up some valuable tricks and tips to make sure every home looks beautiful and alluring to turn the head of a motivated buyer.

If a house is untidy, over-personalised or just poorly presented, you won't be able to get a flattering set of images with which to market it. And, like it or not, this will reflect on you and your agency. An agent is only as good as their listings, and their listings are only as good as their photographs. That's why it's important that you understand how to talk to your client about the presentation of their home, so they understand how it can affect the number of viewings they get and, ultimately, the size of any offer.

Of course, this assumes you know how a home needs to be styled for photography and viewings; if you don't, these pointers should help you to appreciate the basics and find the professional help you may need.

How to make sure every home you list looks stylishly presented

Lose the jargon – Don't talk about home staging; it's unlikely your sellers will have heard the term or know what it means. Instead, call it 'home styling', or 'property styling'. It's a much clearer way of explaining what you are trying to achieve with your guidance and advice.

Be clear with your clients – When you discuss the styling of a client's home, make sure you explain that your aim is to present their house appropriately for photography and viewings. That way, your clients will understand that the styling has a specific purpose and is not just to improve their home – a concept they may find disrespectful. Make sure your clients appreciate that you are not making any kind of judgement about how they live their lives in the house, or their taste in décor. You are seeking to present their home in the best way online so that they achieve the highest level of interest, and therefore viewings, right from the start.

Ask for permission to share your thoughts and ideas with your vendors. Don't just blurt out that they need to repaint their living room. As they show you around their home, ask if you can make suggestions if you see anything that could be tweaked or would be better moved. They will almost always say yes, and then you're not offering unsolicited advice; you have instead sought their permission in advance, and therefore your advice will be received with greater acceptance.

Start small – As you have the tour with the vendor, choose something very small to mention. Perhaps a cushion, or bed linen. Gauge their reaction, and if it's positive and appreciative you can try for a more substantial change, like moving a piece of furniture or pressure-washing a patio. If you go in too strongly with large requests, you risk alienating the client at a potentially delicate stage of your relationship.

Explain what you're doing – When you explain to your client what needs moving, and why, describe any items you don't want in shot as 'distracting'. This way, you're not judging any particular item as being good or bad, just as a distraction on a viewing. Explain that each room has one or two special features, and you want the online browsers to notice these features and remember them – not the African ornament or the full-length nude oil painting. Your clients will be much more receptive to your advice if they understand your reasoning behind it.

Make a list – Have a checklist of anything you need to bring with you on the day of the shoot. Bringing a bouquet of flowers is a nice touch, and we always leave them for the client to keep.

Arrive early – On the day of the photography shoot, arrive at least an hour early to make sure the house is properly prepared for the photographer. If you've built a firm foundation of trust and advice with your client, you should find the house ready. But just in case it isn't, you need to allow plenty of time to make sure the photographs that are captured are the best they could possibly be.

Keep your client close and onside – Make sure the client is going to be present during the photoshoot. I know it's tempting to encourage them to go out, but if you do you're missing a valuable opportunity for them to see exactly how their house needs to be presented for viewings. Also, once they see the images, if they have been absent they may feel mildly (or even strongly) insulted by your moving their furniture and accessories. Best to get buy-in right from the start and begin the relationship on a firm foundation of trust and respect.

Take 'before' photos – Take photos of each room on your phone to remind yourself what needs putting back, where. Also, you can use your phone photos to demonstrate to your client anything that needs moving, and why. It's much easier to explain using a photo than pointing at the room in person.

Take it up a level – bring in a pro

If you're not sure about how the house needs to be styled, or you don't feel confident discussing it with your client, maybe it's time to bring in an expert. Home stagers and property stylists have the skills and experience to deal with difficult situations, challenging vendors and awkwardly presented houses, so let a professional tackle the project. If your fee is generous, perhaps you can absorb their cost into it. If not, get a fixed-fee quote from the stylist and present it to your client. You could agree to add it onto your fee on sale, or if your client is amenable to using a stylist, and appreciates the need for one, they may well agree to cover the fee.

Keep the end in mind; remember why you're going to these lengths, and what result you're hoping for. You want the very best for your client, of course, and a good offer to make it worth all the effort expended; but you also want to show off your client's home, making it look amazing online and in your brochure, so that you can demonstrate your property marketing skills to other valuable vendors.

For a complete list of items to style a photoshoot, please visit: www.samashdown.co.uk/theselectiveagentbook.

Professional copywriting

Take a look at this description:

> The XYZ Estate Agency is proud to offer this REALISTICALLY PRICED opportunity for sale.

That's the way one of our homes was previously described in its headline on Rightmove.

After a few months of little (no) interest, the owner asked us to re-market the apartment. Here's the headline we wrote:

Is this the best location on Windermere?

Which advert would you click on?

The best property descriptions are not always flowery and verbose. Sometimes, getting straight to the point works best. When we do flowery, though, we do it like this:

Rustling up a picnic for a day out on the water? Ripe plums, lemonade and lashings of ginger beer might have sufficed for Julian and co, but if your gastro tastes are a little more demanding, the effortlessly modern kitchen dining room will provide the perfect setting for your epicurean escapades. Brimming with natural light from the many stately sash windows, treat yourself to a lazy morning in your PJs munching toast and reading the Sunday papers in this blissfully open family living room.

Here's how another agent described one of our properties' outdoor space:

There is private parking and a lovely sunny garden area and sunken south-facing patio.

We described it like this:

The garden is a treasure trove of seating areas, sunken patios, hidden paths and bespoke planters, cleverly arranged to create a true haven for birds, butterflies and, of course, you. Watch the sun set over the far-reaching views as the sausages sizzle on the barbeque and you share a bottle of wine next to the chiminea with friends.

Not everyone likes the effusive prose we favour, and that's OK. Our clients – both buyers and sellers – adore it. By offering this level of poetic prose, you will deter sellers who don't value it and who are just looking for a transaction. These are sellers who would be reluctant (or unwilling) to pay your fee and who would therefore be better placed with another agent.

Vendor interview

Our copywriter calls our clients and interviews them for up to an hour. She records the interview and uses it to craft a copy of around 1,000 words. We can then use the parts we need for the brochure and Rightmove. Our clients absolutely love the experience of being interviewed about their house. It makes them feel special, and it allows them to wax lyrical about the home they've probably loved for many years. They talk about what Christmases feel like there, as well as their favourite walks, pubs and restaurants. They tell our copywriter about family time, down time and what they'll miss the most. We get a flavour of what their home means to them, and it helps us to do a better job of selling it to the right buyer – one who will love their home for all the reasons they once fell in love with it.

Magazine-style brochures

Your brochures are going to be your showcase for your new, bespoke marketing and will be the best marketing tools to help you attract and convert the best homes in your area. This means they have to be bold, different, stylish and beautiful. I suggest that you start keeping an 'inspiration collection' – a samples box of brochures you find that you like the look of. Don't stop at brochures either. I've been collecting marketing materials for over fifteen years, and now we have a huge plastic box in the office that no one can move full of direct mail, leaflets, postcards, 'lumpy' mail, torn-out magazine pages, posters, menus and much more. It's a hugely valuable source of inspiration for our brochures (and marketing in general), and we regularly dip in to find just the right colour, style or page layout for a house we're marketing. Start your inspiration collection today and you'll never be stuck for an idea again.

I also use PowerPoint to mock-up any design ideas I have for our designer. Less vital now than it was before we had an in-house designer, it's still a useful way to portray ideas and brief her so she understands what look we're trying to achieve. I've also stuck bits of paper together to signify a fancy fold or format, videoed myself trying to explain it for our designer and printer, and asked a client for a piece of wallpaper from their spare roll in the garage so we can design their brochure around a room they love. Don't be afraid to try something new and different for each house. It will make sure your designer stays interested and invested in the projects you give them; and when you're closely involved and engaged, you'll find it keeps the design process exciting for you, too.

Individual property branding

Our designer creates a unique visual branding for every house we list. Some homes are easier than others to do this for, as their names are more descriptive; for example, 'Rose Cottage' might lend itself to a flowery logo, whereas a name that is more abstract, like 'Ashdown Cottage', will need more imagination.

Printing

Careful property styling, beautiful images and creative design will all be wasted if you choose a cheap printer. Even with exactly the same specifications, print quality varies widely. Look for a printer who will spend the time and care about the finished result just as much as you do. Your brochures are evidence to your clients of your commitment to quality, and you will be judged on them. Specialist print finishes and formats will not only help the home stand out to a buyer; your clients will love them, too. We often have clients asking for extra copies of their brochures to keep and share with their friends.

Bespoke for-sale board

Your designer can create a for-sale board that shows off the house looking its best. If the house is down a drive and not visible from the road, your image needs to showcase the house to grab the attention of drive-bys. If the house is visible from the road, maybe use an image from the bottom of the garden looking back, or a twilight shot, or a drone. Be imaginative, but also let your client be involved in choosing an image that will portray the house looking its best.

Keeping everyone onside

Your freelance team is just that – a team. We hold an annual suppliers' meetup for our freelance team, where we spend time discussing projects, workflows and systems. We find we get valuable feedback from them, and that keeps projects running much more smoothly.

One idea that came out of the last meetup was creating a Facebook group for our whole team – freelancers included. We did this straight away, and now it's full of house videos, floorplans, questions and answers, photography schedules and deadlines, and much more. It's an invaluable part of our bespoke marketing process and we may never have thought of it had it not been for that freelancer's suggestion.

Remember that your freelance team is still a team. Often, freelancers work from home, solo, with little human interaction. Making them feel like valued and important members of your team will help to foster loyalty and trust, and that will make everything you do a lot easier and more enjoyable.

THREE

Cornerstone 1 – Direct Mail

What exactly is direct mail? Is it canvassing or leaflet distribution, or is it those postcards agents love to send?

It's called 'direct' mail for a reason

Direct mail is so called because it's directly addressed to a person or a property. Unlike leaflets, that tend to be sent out indiscriminately door to door (sometimes described as 'canvassing'), direct mail is targeted and is typically sent out in much smaller numbers.

Of course, it's far easier to create a leaflet campaign. Sending out a mailing piece to every single door is much simpler and cheaper per address than picking and choosing the properties that will receive your marketing. But leafleting is also highly ineffective. And, like any marketing activity that is ineffective, that means it's very expensive. An ineffective leaflet campaign will cost you (or your team members) time, energy (sending out 10,000 leaflets takes up mind space as well as floor space in your office – not to mention the environmental impact) and money (the cheaper your leaflets are, the less chance they will return you the result you need and want – and that makes leaflet campaigns very expensive indeed).

Leaflet response rates in the estate agency industry are dire. Whereas a pizza delivery company might only be looking for a sale worth, say, £20, they could get that spend every month for years to come. Thus, their leaflet could be worth thousands of pounds over the next decade or longer. But for an estate agency, the chances of success are much lower. Perhaps 60–70% of people eat pizza, but only around 4% of us move every year. Our window of opportunity, to win someone's attention in between deciding to move and actually putting their home on the market, is actually very small – perhaps only a few weeks.

Because of this, if you are sending out leaflets, it's normal to expect only one response per 10,000 leaflets, which is only a 0.01% response rate. In some areas, agents expect only one or two calls for a batch of 30,000–40,000 leaflets sent out. Not only is this a terrible result for your pocket, it's also pretty dire for our environment. This kind of wastage just is not sustainable, on any level.

Another reason not to use mass leafleting as a form of marketing is that leaflets typically convey an urgent offer of some kind. Deadlines, scarcity and discounting are all very common in leaflet campaigns, and these elements can cheapen your brand, because tactics like these tend to only attract bargain hunters and not the high value homeowners you want to reach.

There's another, bigger problem with leafleting campaigns that may never have occurred to you: what about the other 99.999% of people who received a leaflet from you but didn't actually call you? When you mass leaflet, you damage trust because you're teaching your audience to ignore your marketing. By 'training' the recipients of your marketing to ignore it, eventually they will simply become blind to it. They will look but not see, and soon it simply won't register with them anymore.

If, instead, you are selective in your mailings, and target just a small group of homeowners with a carefully crafted series of letters, your wallet – and the environment – will thank you. Not only that, but the people who receive your mailings will feel they're special by having been targeted specifically, and that makes your piece of direct mail worth so much more to them.

A stamped, handwritten envelope will usually be opened, and anyone who does take the time to read two or even three pages of a well-written letter is far more likely to take an action at the end of it. Having invested a couple of minutes reading and absorbing your content to decide if it's relevant and interesting, they will want to act in alignment with that investment. A leaflet, on the other hand, may take only seconds to digest – just enough time for them to for them to walk across the kitchen and put it in the recycling bin. With no investment of attention or time in reading your message, it's easy for your leaflet to join other 'junk' mail in the recycling, without a second thought.

The 3 Ms of marketing

Before I give you the specific ingredients of a successful direct mail campaign, we need to go back to basics – to the **3 Ms of Marketing**. These are:

Message ➡ Medium ➡ Market

In other words,

What are you asking somebody to do? (Message)

Where and how is your message being shown to them? (Medium)

Who is the message for? (Market)

Without getting all these three foundational elements nailed and ensuring they are each in alignment with your direct mail objectives, your direct mail campaign will fail. I don't want that for you, so let's make sure we get these right, from the off:

Message

Tell your recipient exactly what you want them to do, in the simplest and clearest way possible. Will they understand the action they need to take and feel compelled to do it? Also, is it easy for them to do, or are you asking them to do something that's difficult or time-consuming? Are you asking them to take an action that is just too big a step at this point in your relationship?

If your message is simple, clear and easy to act on, with a reward attached that is commensurate with the effort you're asking them to expend, you are much more likely to achieve the results you are looking for with your direct mail.

Medium

This is what your letter looks like. Many agents are surprised when I tell them that the format you use for your direct mail – and, in fact, in any marketing – is the least important element. Yes, your letter will get a better result if it looks great, but not if you're sending it to the wrong households or including the wrong message. The look and feel of your letter need to be on-brand and attractive, but don't obsess over the design; it's just not as significant as you think it is.

Market

Your choice of recipient is the most important element of the three, by far. It doesn't matter how beautiful your letter, how carefully written and compelling your message, if you're sending your letters to HMOs, empty houses or squats. Choose your roads and areas carefully. Sending out a small number of letters at a time can help you focus your attention on the key areas you want to get known in. We know that boards breed boards, so having a board or two in an affluent area will almost certainly prompt other enquiries from the same area, particularly when your 'sold' slip goes up.

Proof it works

When we launched AshdownJones, my co-director Phil and I knew that our skill in using direct mail was going to be absolutely crucial to the success – or failure – of our new agency, so we became happily obsessed with it. We tried a huge number of different tactics, text, formats and sending sequences, and tested everything. We didn't rest until we could predict almost exactly how many responses we would get to our letters. Having worked with over a thousand independent agents over the last fifteen years, I knew that the benchmark was a response rate of around one in 1,000 for a well-written piece of direct mail, but we were determined to beat that statistic. In fact, we wanted to smash it. And we did.

As we closed our first twelve months of AshdownJones, in April 2018, we calculated that around 70% of all our listed and sold fees were attributable to our direct mail letters. That amounted to approximately £350,000. And we weren't sending them out in big batches, either. Rarely did we send out more than 300 letters in a month, and usually less than 100. Our best response was two valuations (both instructed) out of only six pieces sent out. One of these alone was worth a £16,000 fee to us.

What to say in your direct mail

Only a few years ago, my homeowner consultancy business, HomeTruths, relied 100% on direct mail to generate enquiries. At one point, we were sending out 10,000 hand-addressed, hand-stamped letters every single month. If we got it right, a flood of phone calls would ensue. If we didn't, the phone would remain silent, and all that energy, research and money would be wasted. The stakes were high. Our direct mail budget was often up to £10,000 a month, and mistakes were costly. Not only that, I had a team whose paycheques relied on my creating letters that would work.

I read every book I could get my hands on about direct mail, from the old-school, Madison Avenue days of David Ogilvy, Leo Burnett and Rosser Reeves, through the scientific approaches of Claude C Hopkins and Robert Collier, to the ideas of the fascinating and charismatic Gary Halbert and Dan Kennedy. Dissecting and analysing, I took the many principles I'd learned and tested countless tactics, time and again. Because of the years I spent in the trenches of direct mail marketing, we can now send just a handful of letters from our agency in Windermere to prospective clients and still expect a call or two with quality valuation invites.

In this section, I'm going to share with you my best advice for writing a letter that will get your phone ringing, so you don't have to spend the many years and thousands of pounds that it took me to learn what I now know. For those of you who are reading this and feeling anxious about not being a natural writer, I get it. Most people don't have to write anything as important as sales copy in their working life. But with my help, and a little creative thinking from you, you're going to write a fantastic letter that gets opened, read and acted upon by those clients you want to work with the most. Have a little faith in yourself, because I know you can do it. Ready? Then let's go!

Here's my 'SX20' copywriting system – just follow these twenty tips to get your direct mail written like a pro.

1. Structure

Don't print your letter onto your company letterhead, unless it's a subtle one. Better to just add your company name and address at the top in normal type, so your letter looks more like something they might get from a friend and less like a sales letter. Longer letters have been shown time and time again to outperform short letters, so don't be afraid to let your letter go on to two or more pages. One brilliant copywriter I know regularly sends out eight-page letters, and they work well for him. Test it yourself and see what happens. Yes, most people will give up on page one, but those people who read your letter all the way to the end are your best prospects and are far more likely to take an action after reading.

Add a photo of yourself to your letter so your reader can see who's writing to them. Make it the same as your social media profile photo so they start to get used to seeing your photo and feel you're more familiar to them.

2. Salutation

Don't write 'Dear Homeowner' at the top of your letter. Instead, write a compelling headline in larger font, in the centre. It may look a bit odd in a letter, but I promise you it works.

3. Substance

What is your letter going to be about? What's the main hook? Just like a newspaper story, you need an 'angle' – the point of the letter. Ryan Deiss from DigitalMarketer has a formula he calls the 'gain, logic, fear' sequence.[2] In the first letter (or email, as much of his advice refers to), you'd highlight what your reader will gain by taking the action you propose, in the second, you'll talk about the 'logic' of them taking the next step; then in the 'fear' letter, tell them what they might lose if they don't do anything.

Here is an example of a 'gain, logic, fear' sequence:

Gain: 'Talk to us and make an informed decision'

Logic: 'We sell more houses over £500,000 than any other agent in the area'

Fear: 'You don't want to be the only house on your road that hasn't sold'

4. Sell the sizzle, not the sausage

Don't try to tell your reader everything you know about selling houses in one letter. Remember that you're only trying to get their attention and keep it long enough

---

2   Deiss, R (2015) *The Invisible Selling Machine*. Digital Marketing Labs LLC

for your letter not to end up in the recycling bin. Tell them just enough to tempt them to keep reading, and not so much you blind them with jargon and agent-speak. Keep them reading, wanting to know how the letter ends.

5. Single call to action

What are you asking them to do? Don't suggest they follow you on Facebook, then connect with you on LinkedIn, and read your blog, and maybe, if they have time and they're not too distracted by then, they should pick up the phone for a chat with you. Stop! Just have one call to action, and make it super simple for them to follow.

6. Start with a question

Starting with a question means you're building rapport from the first sentence. You want your reader to be nodding as they read, even if you can't see them. Nodding means you've got their attention because you've asked something that's completely relevant and relatable to them.

7. Select one reader

Who is your ideal client? I want you to imagine them, in detail, in your mind. They could be someone real or someone made up. You need to know their gender, age, life chapter and what's important to them. The more you know about them, the easier it is to write to that singular reader. And when you do that, your letter will become incredibly compelling for that reader; they will feel you know them and understand their situation better than anyone else could.

8. Specificity sells

Talk about their village or even their street. Make your words hyper-specific to them and you'll grab their attention from the first place that they recognise. For example, 'Did you know that homes on Acacia Avenue are selling for 10% higher than they did last year?' is a pretty compelling opener, if you're a resident of Acacia Avenue.

9. Simplicity

Keep your message simple. Remember the old teaching adage: 'Tell them what you're going to tell them, tell them, then tell them what you told them'. Anything important you say in your letter probably bears repeating; just find a new way to say it and a new angle from which to explain it. The clearer you are, the higher the response you will get from your direct mail.

10. Style

Write in a clear, concise style without using lots of long words you wouldn't usually say. (See tip 20, 'Speak like a human', below.) Don't make your sentences too long, either, or you'll lose your readers in a sea of words and they'll give up before they get to the good bit. (There is a good bit in your letter, right?) And don't be afraid to break your school-day grammar rules and start a sentence with an 'and', like this one. It feels natural and encourages the reader to read on, with little effort. For a quick style check, try using the Hemingway App (www.hemingwayapp.com) – a handy little tool that shows you the readability of your prose. Warning: it's a bit addictive.

11. Short sentences

Shorter sentences are easier to read than long ones, and they make the reader feel they're making faster progress. That's why newspapers use columns. And short sentences. Like this.

12. Speak like a human

Use your normal speaking voice; don't try to sound like a corporate robot. Contractions will help you sound like yourself – words like 'can't' instead of 'cannot' and 'don't' in place of 'do not'. They sound more like most people speak, and so they are more familiar and relatable to the reader. Stay clear of the passive voice. 'The house can be found' is passive, whereas 'you'll find the house' is active and sounds more normal.

13. Stories

Telling a (short) story will draw your reader in. Everyone loves a story, and they are easier and more enjoyable to read than standard statements of facts. Choose a story that is directly relevant to your reader and that ties in to the action you want them to take. Perhaps it's a story about how you styled a house for £50 and sold it within a week. Or maybe you have a great tale about someone whose house you sold when all other agents had failed, and how you helped their family move on to their dream home. Make your story interesting and emotional, with your client as the hero and you as their guide, so your reader can imagine themselves in the same situation.

14. Emotions

You can use emotions in your copy to draw the reader in and meet them where they are in their emotional journey. I've listed some emotions here, together with an example of how you might use each one in your sales letter:

- Belonging – Feeling a part of your team or part of a community of other homeowners like them

- Hope – Instilling a feeling of hope and empowerment that they will be able to sell and move on with their lives

- Guilt – You can gently pull their guilt strings if they feel they are not doing the best for their family by not being able to sell their home and move on

- Vanity – Flatter them in their choice of current home, and make them feel they make smart and educated decisions

- Fear – Gently tap into any concerns they may have about not moving, like losing a job offer or their dream house

- Lust – What is it your ideal client desires most? Show them the lifestyle they want, and demonstrate how achievable it is with your help and advice

- Greed – Don't be scared to talk about the money your reader wants to earn from selling their home; appeal to their natural aspiration to want more than they currently have

15. Steal from the pros

Take a leaf out of a scriptwriter's box of tricks and try a story 'loop'. This is when you start a story and then leave it unfinished, only concluding it at the end of the letter. Adding 'but more on that story later...' or a similar cliff-hanger will keep your reader reading all the way to the end to find out what happened – so your story better have a good ending!

16. Sell benefits not features

It's a cliché (because it's true) that no one wants to buy a drill; they want a hole. In fact, they probably want a shelf, or something similar. Don't try to sell a drill to people who just want a shelf. Sell the outcome, not the process. Don't tell them how you operate, in a blow-by-blow account, just ask them to imagine how it will feel when they are living in the house of their dreams. If you do describe something you do (a feature) make sure you back it up with a phrase like 'which means that' (a benefit).

17. Show proof

Case studies and examples of your successes, including statistics, will add credibility to your letter. Give your reader a short background to a case study, explain what you did to change the situation, and then reveal the results, with figures (time and money, usually).

18. Spell out the next step

Make sure that your reader knows exactly what they need to do next. Spell it out for them, even if it seems obvious to you. For example, if you've asked them to call in to the office, tell them who in your team is most likely to answer, when your opening hours are and what the result of their phone call will be. People are drawn to certainty and move away from the unknown, so make them feel reassured that they know exactly what will happen when they take the action you have asked them to take.

19. Seek a second opinion

Even if you think you're a great writer (I'm sure you are), a spelling or grammar mistake may have slipped by both you and Spellcheck, so ask someone you trust to read it to make sure it's accurate and free of typos.

20. Say it out loud

I use this little technique with everything I write, and I never fail to change something. When you read your own copy out loud, you hear where the flow is broken and where you trip over a tricky sentence structure. Reading out loud and changing those awkward phrasings will take your letter from good to brilliant in just a few minutes.

Your direct mail checklist

I've created for you a distilled checklist of general principles so your direct mail brings you new, quality leads for your agency.

✔ **No more sending mass leaflets, ever!** – From now on, it's targeted direct mail all the way.

✔ **Keep branding to a minimum** – Keep it looking like a letter with plain black text.

✔ **Use white or cream-coloured paper** – not coloured or patterned.

✔ **Keep your envelope unbranded and white or cream** – A plain DL or C5 is fine. And don't spend money on high-quality envelopes – the testing we've done shows it makes zero difference to your results.

✔ **Take the time to handwrite the address** – If you don't have neat handwriting (and I definitely don't), allocate the task to a team member who does.

✔ **Use a stamp** – not a franking machine. Stamped envelopes get a much higher open rate.

✔ **Name your letters** so that, in the future, you can identify the good ones and the ones that weren't so successful. Print them all out with the name of the letter at the top, and keep them in a binder for easy reference.

✔ **Add a PS** – It's been often proven that people read the headline and the end of a letter, and only then do they go back and read the body if they are interested enough to invest the time. It doesn't matter what the PS is, just so long as you include one; a repetition of a key phrase or call to action is fine.

✔ **Don't use a salutation on the envelope** – Any letter addressed to 'The Homeowner' is unlikely to be opened, as people will assume it's just junk mail (which your letter most definitely is not). Instead, only write the address on the envelope, and it will be impossible to ignore.

ARENA: A handy formula for writing a great letter

Starting your letter is always the hardest part. Years ago, I created a formula to help me get past that pesky first paragraph and into the meaty bit. And because it's a step-by-step formula, following it will make sure you don't miss anything important, like the call to action. (Believe me, people have done exactly that.)

It's also a handy mnemonic (which is just a fancy name for a group of letters that spell something to help you remember the sequence): ARENA. Here's what it means:

Affinity

Reassure

Explain or easy win

Nutshell

Action

This is how the formula works when you're writing your letter:

Affinity – 'Are you feeling frustrated that all the other houses in your village seem to be selling, while yours is still on the market?'

Reassure – 'You're not alone. Many other homeowners in your village have already been in touch to find out what they can do to sell their homes more effectively.'

Explain or easy win – 'I'm going to take you through our easy, 5-point checklist to see if there's anything you can do yourself to help generate more interest in your house, so you can move on with your life.'

Nutshell – 'As you can see, by following our 5-point checklist, you'll be in a much better position to figure out why you're not getting viewings and offers – and what you can do to change that.'

Action – 'If you'd like independent feedback on your Rightmove advert, we'd love to help. Just drop us a line on _____ and we can have a confidential chat about your best options to get you moving.'

Here's how a letter about 'downsizing' might look:

'Are you wondering whether you should downsize, but you're not sure how to go about it? If you love your house and your neighbours, and you feel a real sense of community where you are, you may be reluctant to move house. On the other hand, perhaps your house is just too big for you, with too many rooms you don't use. Maybe you have a big garden you need to spend time or money maintaining.

It's perfectly natural to be feeling conflicting emotions about a decision to move or stay. Over the last two decades, we have helped thousands of people to make the right decision for them, and because of this we know that once the decision is made it becomes easier. The anticipation of moving home is often worse than the reality.

Downsizing is often a very positive move, freeing up valuable funds and time. Living in a smaller home that fits you better means less worry, more time and an ability to do those things that you've always wanted to do.

We've found that when someone is making the difficult decision to downsize, they find it helpful to discuss it with us before taking any action. Just a confidential chat over a cup of tea, so they can ask us questions and better understand their options.

Once you can make an informed decision about your next move, downsizing can be an exciting and enjoyable experience. Just give us a call on _____ and take the first step towards making the right decision for you.'

This is a shorter letter than we'd usually send, but it demonstrates how you can use the ARENA structure in a real letter format. Feel free to use this letter idea, and add in a case study or a story of how you've helped someone downsize. You could also include facts and statistics about downsizing or a quote from research in the media. You could also write a digital guide, sometimes called an 'e-book', and link to it in your letter. With a complex and often emotional subject like 'downsizing', your readers will be interested in as much information as possible. This is your chance to position yourself as the expert on downsizing, and it all begins with your letter, so make it a good one.

Who to send your direct mail to

Before you prepare your direct mailing, you need to decide whether you're going to send your letters to houses that are on the market already with other agents or to those that are not currently for sale. Your decision will have an important implication for the content of your letter, so you need to choose one route or another at the outset. Write carefully with your reader in mind; if they're already struggling to sell, they need to hear a different message from you than if they have no intention to move in the foreseeable future.

There's also little point in sending your carefully crafted letters to every single house in your area. You need to be selective. Unless you have unlimited funds and time (highly unlikely if you're an independent estate agent), you need to focus your investment on a small number of houses: I suggest you send no more than 500 letters out at any one time, but start off by experimenting with smaller batches of 250 or less. Once you know what you've written gets responses, you can afford to roll out your direct mail campaign over a larger area, knowing it's a safer bet than a letter you have not yet tested.

Your direct mail needs to be a system

Direct mail is not just something you need to do when things are quiet or when your stock is low. To ensure that your direct mail letters get sent out frequently and consistently, you need a system: a written schedule of which addresses will receive which letters, on what dates, and sent by which person in your organisation. Ideally, this won't be you, but if you're just starting out and don't yet have staff, then this is your opportunity to create and perfect your direct mailing schedule so you can more easily delegate it when you are ready to recruit. The schedule and system is vital because it means that no matter what else is happening, your direct mail is creating fresh, new leads for you, every week of every month, ad infinitum.

Successful direct mail campaigns are built on consistency and frequency; they are not a one-off activity. My clients who have a robust direct mail system and a schedule they stick to get fantastic results; and you will too, if you follow my guidelines. Don't re-invent the wheel – learn from my mistakes and short-cut to a successful direct mail strategy that brings in new high value clients every single week!

If you'd like to know more about how we could help you with your direct mail, go to http://bit.ly /bookacallwithsam and book a call with me.

FOUR

Cornerstone 2 – Premium Content That Drives Targeted Traffic

You've probably heard people like me tell you that you need 'content' for your business. But what is content and why do you need it?

In this chapter, I'll tell you exactly what content is, why it's so important to the growth of your agency and how to create it.

Firstly, let's look at what content *is*. A blog post can be content, but so can a:

- Video

- Checklist

- Article

- Letter

- Slide deck

- Infographic

- How-to guide

- Podcast

- Information page on your website

And much more. Anything you create that informs, persuades or entertains your audience is content. Your content strategy is something that should be unique to you and should fit your brand. There's little point in me telling you to create video, for example, if you hate being on camera. But video can be a great alternative to writing a blog post if you're not someone who finds constructing written content easy.

Even though your content strategy needs to be right for you, you do need to create both written and visual content. The best way to do this is by having a substantial (1,000 words plus) blog post published on your website at least monthly. Once you have this, you can create other types of content around it, with each one driving more visitors to your site.

Why create content?

There are so many reasons why you need to create content that I should dedicate a whole book to the topic. (Perhaps I will, one day.) For now, I'm going to give you five reasons why creating quality, original content is vital for your business, and how it will help propel your agency to another level of brand awareness and success.

Reason #1 – It strengthens brand awareness

Creating and distributing content creates – and builds upon – brand awareness. Your brand will get noticed in lots of different places, and on several channels. When people see your branded content over and over again, the familiarity they feel with your brand becomes fondness, and eventually trust.

Reason #2 – It positions your website as the go-to resource for your target audience

Quality content that answers your audience's questions will also boost your SEO. This means when somebody Googles, say, 'How to sell my house faster', your blog post will be there on page one of Google – or, that's the theory. In practice, there are a few technical elements you need to get right on your website before this can happen; but if you create high-quality, consistent content that genuinely answers the questions your audience ask, you should start seeing your website rank higher and higher in the search results.

Reason #3 – It builds your audience

On average, around 3% of all properties in the UK are for sale, and another 12% of homeowners are considering moving in the next couple of years. This means you have a 15% opportunity to talk to those people currently on the market or soon to be. When you create the right content (more on this to come), you'll attract an audience, 15% of whom could be your target market – ie, people on, or considering going on, the market. Instead of trying to find and pursue those homeowners who are on the market right now, create content that will attract the right people and they will come to you. Then all you need to do is to build a bigger audience.

Reason #4 – It builds trust

Estate agency is a trust industry; arguably more so than most other industries. Often, however, our industry is portrayed as one to mistrust. I believe (time to get on my soap box) that we have a real opportunity here to change that perception – indeed, a responsibility to do so. If we have a poor reputation, who else is there to blame but ourselves? The right content can help us portray the true 'us': likeable, trustworthy, friendly, helpful, expert, experienced and caring. Quality content enables you to become more transparent, which, in turn, builds trust.

Reason #5 – It positions you as a thought leader

Do you want to be seen as a progressive and innovative thought leader? As someone who is not afraid to be proactive, in an industry that is known for being reactive? Content will help you to do that. Your content is just that – yours. You can be opinionated while educating, and so long as you are respectful and considerate in your argument you will be admired for your content. People are drawn to thought leaders and influencers, and those who are not afraid to take a stand for their beliefs and values. We're attracted to those people who we feel are influencers, who have the latest ideas and who want to share their ideas in a non-dictatorial way – in a fun, engaging and entertaining way. And that's what you can do with your content.

Let's talk about awareness

Does anyone know who you are? Have they heard of your brand? Brand awareness matters because if no one knows who you are, you'll find it a challenge to not only charge what you're truly worth but also to get the enquiry in the first place. In this chapter, I'm going to take you through the steps to create the right quality content to make sure you're getting noticed, for all the right reasons. But first, let's look at the 'Five Phases of Awareness™' and how this journey can affect your enquiries, conversion and fees.

Phase One: Zero Awareness – This is when nobody has a clue who you are, and they've never heard of your brand. You often inhabit this phase for a prolonged period when you're a new agency and you have to rely on aggressive touting practices, as well as begging for joint instructions, to even get your agency off the ground. You see no choice but to undercharge and overpromise. Phase one is not an enjoyable place to be, but the good news is that the right content strategy can help you graduate from this phase.

Phase Two: Low Awareness – Here, you're still struggling for brand awareness and so you only get invited out to the low-quality instructions, where you're competing on fee. You're probably seduced into overvaluing, and you're still not converting well. This is a challenging phase, but a well-planned content strategy can lift you out of this phase quickly and effectively.

Phase Three: Medium Awareness – At last, you're starting to be considered as a credible alternative to the better-known agents. You're finally getting invited out to some nice properties, you're holding a better level of fee, and you're starting to convert at 40%, 50% or more. You're beginning to see the light at the end of the tunnel, but you've only just started because even better is around the corner. You're about to enter…

Phase Four: High Awareness – You are now their favourite agent. They thought of you first when they decided to put their house on the market and you're often the first one through the door. Your fee is much less important to this client than your service, your values and your integrity. In this phase, you may be surprised to notice that even though you're quoting a higher fee, you're converting more often, frequently at two out of three, and higher. You're starting to see the success that you hoped for.

But the best is yet to come, in...

Phase Five: Prime Choice – It's finally happened. You are the only agent through the door. Your fee is almost irrelevant because it's you they want. No other agent has even been given a look-in. Your confidence is high; your fees, even higher, and your business is the strongest it's ever been. Well done!

Bridging the 'Trust Gap'

To move from the early phases of awareness, where you are largely relying on your fee and promises to convert, to the High Awareness and Prime Choice phases, where you are the default agent for the homeowner, you need to move past the 'Trust Gap'.

The 'Trust Gap' is a barrier, one that you need bridge. Beyond it is the promised land, where your clients stop instructing you on your valuation and fee, and instead instruct you because they love your brand, your values and, most importantly, you.

A Trust Gap exists because your client is on a journey: it's the Know-Like-Trust-Try-Buy journey,[3] and they need to go through each of these steps in order, to get to the feeling that they have to 'buy' you because they buy into you, and they know that you 'get' them, too. That deep-seated connection makes it so much easier to work with these clients, and you can achieve this connection through your content marketing.

But how do you achieve awareness when, as we know, most advertising doesn't work?

Of course you want to be an amazing agency. You want your staff to be amazing. You want your brand and your delivery services to be amazing. But it's hard to be amazing every single day and you will, at times, drop the ball. And that's because you're juggling. You're going to forget to send that email or return that phone call. You're going to go to a house with the wrong keys. Do all of those make you a bad estate agent? No. But being useful is an easier goal to pursue, and to prove, through your content marketing.

---

3   Jantsch, J (2011) *Duct Tape Marketing*. Thomas Nelson

Prediction marketing

Prediction marketing is about anticipating your audience's needs and questions so you can create content that is ready for them, when they need it.

It's simple. All you need to do is answer their Googled questions in your content. That way, you become top of mind before they decide to sell, and, therefore, their choice of agent when they sell. The 'when' here is very important, because great content marketing is not about 'pushing' someone along the journey and trying to persuade them to take the next step. It's much more passive; it's about your relevant content being ready and waiting for them, when they need it. In other words, when they are searching for the answer to their questions, at each stage of their thought process, your content is there to inform and guide them, so they can move through their own personal journey at a speed that feels most comfortable to them.

Your clients' lifetime moving journey

Apparently, we move around six to ten times in our lifetime. (Not me; I'm on my 46th and planning my 47th move as I write.) Most people move out from living with their parents into a flat, or a small terraced home, or perhaps a rental. Then, as time goes by and their earning power increases, maybe they buy their first property. It'll be something modest in size, so it probably doesn't take long for them to start feeling squeezed, especially if they start a relationship and begin living as a couple.

A natural upwards move from this would be into a three-bed semi, and perhaps they stay in this house for several years. If they decide to have a family, they may well be able to make their three-bed semi work for a while. But once their family begins to grow, and they run out of space, they're ready to upsize again.

Perhaps they decide to move to a four-bed home on an estate, something with a bit more parking and garden space, and they'll probably be happy here for a few years, maybe more. Some people never move from this property stage, while others keep climbing upwards, and sometimes sideways, as job offers, school catchments and life's little curveballs, trigger all sorts of unexpected changes in situation.

Those who do move upwards from this house are usually seeking their 'forever home'. An improvement in the family finances through an inheritance or bonus may mean they can now buy the home they've always dreamed of: perhaps that barn conversion with land, or the old vicarage. Now is the time when they can make that dream happen, and this is likely where they will stay until they become our downsizers, in twenty years, ready to move back down the chain again.

Knowing exactly where your ideal client is on their journey means you can align your content with them at each step they take.

Step 1 - Identify your ideal client

Your ideal client is one who is a good fit for you and your agency. Someone who will be a pleasure to deal with over the coming weeks and months, and whose house is wonderful enough to add prestige to your property register. Perhaps you're thinking of an actual client right now, one who was genuinely grateful for all your help with their property sale, who valued your advice and who actually followed it. The one whose calls you are happy to take because they were always so enthusiastic about all you did for them. Do you have that person in your mind? Good. If you don't have a particular client in your mind, could your ideal client be a composite of several clients? Perhaps you had a wonderful, grateful, joy-to-work-with client who had a house that wasn't especially great. And another who had a gorgeous house but didn't fit the easy-to-work-with criteria. Take their best attributes, and write them down; this is the person you're going to aim to attract via your content marketing strategy.

First-time sellers – These homeowners have never sold a home before, and therefore they don't yet know what can go wrong. They have not yet had a sale fall through or had a property undervalued on survey. They've never been gazumped or gazundered, and they may not even know that these strange events can occur. In fact, most first-time sellers will assume that once they put their home on the market, they'll have an immediate flurry of viewings and be able to take their pick of the offers that come in, and that their sale will progress to completion without incident.

These are the people who will question your fee because they don't know what you do for it. They usually assume that all you do is 'stick it on Rightmove'. They don't want – or need – a full-service estate agent, and therefore they will often simply use a DIY agent, like Purplebricks or Yopa. The idea of paying £700 or £800, instead of 1%, will be very attractive to them. And that's fine. These people are not your clients. Leave them to the DIYs.

Downsizers – At the other end of the selling cycle are the downsizers. These are the homeowners who have been considering selling for years. You may well have been asked to give them an up-to-date appraisal on their home from time to time, or even annually. They don't want to move, but they know they should move. Their children have fled the nest and probably all have their own families by now.

Our downsizers are rattling around in houses that are simply too big for them. Their families are trying to persuade them to downsize sooner rather than later, as perhaps the stairs and the garden are both becoming a bit of a challenge for them. They are likely to be in their late sixties or early seventies and often have lived in their home for a couple of decades or more. Downsizers are emotionally invested in their home, and that attachment is hard to break. Even if they do eventually put their home on the market, it may well be at too high a price because what have they got to lose? If they don't sell, they get to stay in the home they love. And often, even if an asking price offer comes in, they can take ages to consider it and then panic because they don't have anything to move into. And that's your next challenge, because if your downsizers don't find the perfect property – one that is half the size and half the price of their current home but still fits all their furniture – then they're not going anywhere, so the sale will be off. And while they may have been willing to pay your fee without haggle, it's all hypothetical because you may never get the chance to charge it.

Aspiring family – In between these two very challenging types of vendors is the aspiring family. Typically, they'll have moved at least once or twice before, so they know the score. And, as a busy family, they're looking for service, not the cheapest fees. They're prepared to pay for peace of mind, minimal hassle and the right for-sale board outside their door. For simplicity's sake, we call these folks 'Tom' and 'Claire', and here's what we know about them:

They drive an Audi or BMW, shop at Waitrose and Sainsbury's, (not in Lidl and Aldi), and they like brands like The White Company, John Lewis and Jo Malone. They go on holiday to Tuscany and Provence and go skiing. And they're more likely to watch *Planet Earth* than *The X Factor*. They have successful careers, young-ish children and a good circle of friends. Crucially, they would never consider choosing a professional service provider from a leaflet. A pizza company, yes. But they wouldn't select a solicitor, accountant or stockbroker from a DL leaflet, so why would they choose an estate agent from one? That's the bad news. Now for the good news: These folks do use social media, which makes them easy – and cost-effective – to reach. Claire, in particular, loves Facebook and Instagram. She keeps up to date with all her friends' and family's news through her newsfeed several times a day. Because of this, she's open to interesting and entertaining information from brands she knows and trusts. And your aim is to be one of those brands.

Once you've identified your ideal client, creating relevant and interesting content, and broadcasting that content to the right audience, becomes so much easier. And next time some nice person asks you to advertise in the parish magazine, you can ask yourself, 'Do Tom and Claire read this?' and there you have your answer.

At AshdownJones, our ideal clients are Tom and Claire – our upsizing family. If you don't yet have your ideal client firmly in mind, this next exercise will help.

1. Take a pen and paper, list the last five clients you were instructed by, and tick any you felt not only aligned with your brand values but were also enjoyable to work with. Which ones appreciated your value and followed your advice?

2. Write down everything you know about them: age, gender, marital status, holidays, occupation, income, kids, pets, favourite brands, shops and cars. If there's anything you don't know, take an educated guess.

3. List what you think are the best ways to reach them. What marketing do you think these people respond to? For example, we know that our Tom and Claire don't respond to leaflets – at least, not for professional services – but they will respond to a well-written letter. Ask yourself, would they respond to a radio advert, social media post, Facebook advert, community sponsorship or invitation to an event? Create a list of all the marketing channels you can think of, and tick the ones you think best suit your ideal client and which are the most likely to elicit a response from them.

4. Imagine you're eavesdropping on a conversation between your ideal client and someone close to them, such as their partner or friend. You hear them say, 'I really want to move, but...' What's the rest of that sentence? Write down all the different possibilities that might prevent them from moving home. Include objections like cost, time, effort and anything else you can think of. Here are some examples from our Tom-and-Claire list:

'I really want to move, but I'm not sure when would be the best time.'

'I really want to sell the house, but I'm worried I won't find something I love.'

'I really want to move, but I'm not sure if we can afford it.'

This 'But' list is going to help you to create relevant, timely, helpful content that completely aligns with your ideal client's journey, both now and as they take each step towards their move.

The conversations that your ideal client is having – right now – are the fuel for your content marketing strategy. If you can join the conversation already happening in that person's mind, and create content around this, your ideal client will be drawn to you. They'll see you as not just the best agency to help them but as the only agency that can help them with their specific moving or property challenge. Anything you create that helps you connect with your ideal client – be it blogs, articles, e-books, checklists, videos, infographics, or anything else – means that you can prove to them, over and over again, that you understand their needs better than anyone else. And that is hugely powerful for your agency.

Step 2 – Create content that they will love

Great content is telling, not selling. You're inform-ing, helping, educating and guiding, while being entertaining and interesting to your reader. Although this may sound like a daunting challenge, just take the steps in this book, and put your heart and soul into creating the very best content for your ideal client, and your content will act as an attraction magnet. And the great news is that, unless your competitors are also reading this book, you have a valuable opportunity to create a content library and begin attracting new clients before your competitors even notice what you're doing.

What are they Googling?

Once you know who your ideal client is, and what's important to them, you can take an educated guess at the questions they are googling around their home move. Knowing this will help you to create your content focusing on the answers to the questions they have in their heads and that crop up in their private conversations. They will feel that you've read their minds...which, in a way, you have!

Here's how to find out what they are googling: go to Google and type in a broad search, like: 'How to sell a house'. As you type in your search text, you'll see that Google auto-suggests some other searches. Make a note of these alternative searches as you do your research; there are usually another four to eight of them. Here are the alternative searches that Google suggested for me:

- How long will it take to sell my house

- How to sell a house in Scotland

- How to sell a house fast

- How to sell a house privately

- How to sell a house UK

Click 'Enter' to have Google perform the search. Once the search is complete, just below the sponsored listing results at the top of the page you'll see the 'Featured Snippets' section of the search results. This is a summary of an answer to your search query, taken from a webpage, plus a link to that page. It's the answer Google has determined to be the best available one, using their secret algorithm. This means you can't request for your page to be featured in this section; however, you can use the information there to guide your content, so that yours shows up as high as possible in the rankings.

Next, you'll see the 'People also ask' section. This is a series of questions with a drop-down answer for each. The ones that came up for me in my Google search of 'How to sell a house' were:

- What are the costs in selling a house?

- What are the closing costs for a seller?

- What should I do before selling a house?

- What sells a house fast?

- What fees can I expect when selling a house?

- How much tax do you pay when selling a house?

You'll see the question about 'closing costs' isn't relevant to a UK audience, although if you have a large ex-pat audience in your area it could be a relevant topic for you to create content about.

Next, look at the very bottom of the page of Google search results, where you'll see a section called 'Searches related to how to sell a house' with eight further alternate search suggestions. Here are mine:

- How to sell a house UK

- Selling your house tips

- Selling my house what do I need to know

- Selling your house quickly

- Selling house viewing tips

- Selling a house costs

- How to present your house for sale

- How to sell your house without an estate agent

If you follow this process, you'll end up with around twenty Google questions, including your original one. You may find that some more specific or obscure search terms won't prompt the Featured Snippets or the 'People also ask' sections, but all should show some auto-complete suggestions as you type in the search bar as well as the 'Searches related to...' section at the bottom. This means you'll now have several questions you can create content for – and not just blogs, but other content, too, like videos and checklists – knowing that your ideal client is searching for these specific answers.

How Google sends visitors to your content

Type 'Sell your home with social media' into the Google UK search box, and you'll see that my blog is on the first page of the results. As I write this, it ranks second in the organic results. I use an 'incognito' browser window when I search for it, to ensure my preferences (ie, visiting my own site regularly) are not remembered by Google. I also checked today for the search queries 'How to get more viewings on your house' (seventh organic result) and 'Do I need a for-sale sign' (third). If you blog consistently and frequently – monthly, at least – Google will reward you by sending visitors to your website if they have typed in a question or search term that Google thinks you have the answer to. This means that if you write content that a) aligns with the moving journey of your ideal client, b) gives them the answers and information they seek, and c) covers the topic better than the other search results, you'll see your content ranking higher and higher in the search results.

Your website visitor numbers

You'll need Google Analytics on your website to monitor your site visitors. If you don't already have your code installed, you may need to ask your web developer to do this on your behalf. Google Analytics will only track forward from the day you install it; it can't report backdated results, so it's important that you get it installed as soon as possible. Once it's installed, you'll be able to view a fascinating amount of information about your site visitors, including the content on your site they like best, which sites they have come from and how long they stay on an individual page. There are many YouTube tutorials on how to use the data on Google Analytics; they'll show you everything you need to know about using this vital business tool.

The right way to write your first blog post

Enough procrastination – it's time to write your first blog post. No more excuses, urgent tasks getting in the way or staring blankly at a blinking cursor on an empty screen. You can do this, with my help, even if you've never written so much as a thank-you card before. Let's do it together.

Decide on your blog post length – This should be 750 words minimum. Someone can read a 750-word blog post in around three minutes, so it's not the *War and Peace* you're probably thinking it is. Aim for 750, and if you are still writing as you approach 1,000, give yourself a big pat on the back. I suspect once you start writing you'll find your style and momentum. It's the starting that is the hard part.

Decide on your blog post topic – If you've followed the steps earlier in this chapter, you should have some ideas about what topic to write your blog post on. If not, I'm going to suggest that you write your first blog post on the subject of 'presenting your home for sale'. There are several reasons to choose property presentation as your first topic: property presentation posts are usually the most popular, you already know your stuff without having to do tons of research (you know more than you think you do), and if you make it a 'list' post you'll find it pretty easy to write. Trust me.

Sketch out your blog post plan – This is best done with a pen and paper. Just write (in note form) a short introduction, then a list of what you plan on including, then a summary or conclusion. Here's one I made earlier, about a blog post called 'Seven steps to get your house ready for a viewing':

- You may be worried about how your home looks to a buyer

- It's important to get your home looking nice

- Simple steps can make preparation for a viewing easy

- Grab a washing basket and put into it everything that doesn't belong where you found it

- Remove all pet paraphernalia

- Clear all surfaces and floors

- Plain white bedding

- Empty bins and move washing

- Open windows to air and light scented candles

- Get yourself ready with a smile

- As you can see, just follow our seven steps

- Turn a viewer into a buyer

- If you need a chat about how your home might look to a viewer ... [phone number]

How easy was that? Once you have your structure, my suggestion (and this works for me) is to start writing the list, then the conclusion, and then go back and write the introduction. I often don't have a clue what headline to give my post until I've written it, so don't worry if you don't know either. Just get writing, and you'll be pleasantly surprised at how the rest just seems to fall in place.

If you're struggling with the actual writing of your blog post, but you know your content and what you want to say, try dictating your post into your phone if it has a voice recording feature (such as the handy native Voice Memo app for iPhones). Just speak your ideas into your phone – maybe out on a dog walk or in the car – and type them into a Word document. There's even an online transcription service available called www.Rev.com that charges US$1 per minute. You only need around ten minutes for a decent-length blog post, so it could be the best $10 you've ever spent.

A final word on content

Content is the new marketing. Seriously, I can't think of a single type of business that would not benefit from quality content marketing published and distributed on a consistent basis. Estate agency has a wealth of potential material – and a ready audience, eager to consume it. Our industry is often misunderstood and the services we provide undervalued. Content marketing gives you the chance to tell the world what you do and how you do it, and to help people move on in every way.

If you'd like to know more about how we could help you with your content, go to http://bit.ly/bookacallwithsam and book a call with me.

FIVE

Cornerstone 3 – Digital Marketing Funnels

Digital marketing is simply online marketing. But instead of getting hung up on the tools and technology you think you'll need to get digital marketing working for you, I want you to think instead of digital marketing in terms of the journey you want your audience to take. For example, can you show them an article on Facebook that then takes them to your website, which in turn motivates them to call you? Or maybe you can email them a link to a guide that only some of your email subscribers will be attracted to, and therefore you'll be able to create a small list of people you know are interested in a particular subject.

A marketing funnel is a tool that shows how someone responds to your marketing, taking them on the journey from being a stranger to a client.

Of course, not everyone will make the complete journey; some people may read a blog post you've written then disappear forever. Others may love your post so much they seek out more, before going on to check out and like your Facebook page, watch your videos and download your free guide. Once they are smitten, it's a small step for them to pick up the phone and arrange a valuation of their home with you. And given how 'warm' they are now, having consumed all your content before booking the valuation, they are much more likely to instruct you and not one of your competitors.

- A stranger to you comes across your content, your Facebook page or a letter from you – KNOW

- They take an action – maybe liking a Facebook post or downloading a checklist – LIKE

- You have a conversation with them by email or phone – TRUST

- They book a valuation – TRY

- They instruct you – BUY

The former stranger has taken a journey with you, nurtured at each step.

The best content conversion funnels have four moving parts:

1. Subscriber briber

2. Landing page

3. Email nurture sequence

4. Traffic

Step 1 – create a subscriber briber. This should be something valuable that will motivate a prospective client to give you their email address in exchange for it. It could be an e-book or a checklist; make it relevant for the market you want to attract.

Step 2 – take them to a dedicated page. There's no point in driving website traffic to your home page; there are simply too many distractions on it for them to notice your freebie and click on it. Create a distraction-free zone for your freebie, called a 'squeeze page', and your conversion rate will skyrocket.

Step 3 – send them a sequence of automated emails. These must be emails that your readers will love to receive. Add them to your email service provider and you have an automated 'touch campaign' to keep you top of mind. This is just a series of information-rich emails, in a scheduled sequence, designed to build on the relationship you have begun with your subscriber.

Step 4 – drive traffic – both paid and organic (eg, Facebook ads and a 'pillar' blog post). At the time of writing, Facebook ads have risen sharply in price over the last few months, so make sure you know what you're doing so you don't burn through cash, or enlist an expert. A 'pillar' post is a substantial and professionally written blog post that positions you as an expert and creates motivation in the reader to take the next step.

In this section, we'll explore the main components of digital marketing: social media, email marketing, digital assets and paid traffic.

Social media

Social media can be a minefield – a scary, dangerous place. But don't worry, I'm here to be your social media guide and to get you safely and effectively to the other side, where an abundance of new clients awaits.

What content works on social media

I'm going to share my secret formula for choosing what to post on social media. I created it years ago and have been refining and testing it ever since. It's effective and surprisingly simple, and it's called 'Sam's BLAST Formula'.

My BLAST Formula works a bit like a diet. You can post outside this formula, just as you can have a treat every now again when you're on a diet. But if you are constantly eating treats and forgetting your fruit and veggies, your diet is not going to work. It's the same with the BLAST Formula. A few posts every now and again outside your BLAST Formula isn't going to hurt your following or social reach, but if your BLAST posts are in the minority, or you aren't using the formula every day, you're not going to get the results that you want and that are entirely possible – if not probable – with the right strategy.

Sam's BLAST Formula consists of:

Behind the scenes

Local spotlight

A day in the life

Showcase of a property

Tips and advice

Let's explore each one of these in turn, and I'll show you how you can use them to grow your social media following and engagement:

Behind the Scenes – This is the most important of the BLAST elements; people love seeing behind the curtain of an estate agency. Here are some of our recent posts that did well:

- Our designer working on a watercolour painting for a brochure
- A photo of our photographer standing in a bath, going the extra mile to get the perfect shot
- Unboxing our latest bespoke brochures, fresh from the printer's
- Phil taking in the view on a valuation visit (which could also be a 'sneak peek' post)

Local spotlight – connect with your local businesses and give them any support you can. It will come back to you in spades. For us, this has been in the form of:

- An afternoon office run to our favourite café for brownies
- A competition with a local florist
- A 'pay it forward' initiative with five local eateries
- An interview with the owner of a new shop in our town
- Photos of two of our team helping someone who had dropped his car keys in the lake

A day in the life – This is you and your team, doing whatever you do when you're not being an estate agent. Here's what we've posted recently:

- Live from a local river that had burst in recent heavy rainfall

- A photo of a plant I came across while walking in Scotland, and how I asked what it was (turned out to be curly kale)

- A live video of a water-logged car in a local flash flood

- A full rainbow one morning on the way into the office

Showcase of a property – Be careful with property adverts – any social media platform will restrict the reach your post receives if it seems you're posting ads. Try instead: a 'sneak peek' of a property coming soon, a 'new to market' post or even a 'just sold' post. Some ideas from our most popular Showcase posts:

- The initials of a famous local, carved into the stones on a house over a hundred years ago

- A bath with a view, from a house coming to market soon

- Live from a twilight shoot (could also be a 'behind the scenes' post)

Tips and advice – From the tiniest household hack, to the most in-depth video Q&A, your audience will lap up your advice and consider you an expert. Here's how we do it:

- A live 'Ask AJ' video discussing '7 reasons to sell your house in spring'

- The link to our blog on the same topic

- Sam on a live video testing some sticker removal tricks from a bathroom suite

And that's my BLAST Formula. It's not hard to follow, but it's important that you stick to it. Just get into the habit of posting frequently and consistently, and be patient. I promise you, this will grow your local, relevant followers – one person, and post, at a time.

Which platforms should you use?

You literally have hundreds to choose from. Wikipedia has a running list of the major active social networking sites, which as of the time of writing numbers is 212. Deciding to have an active presence on lots of social media sites will stretch your resources beyond their limit, I would suggest. And, no, I don't advocate auto-posting from social media management platforms. You need to spend your limited time and attention on a small number of sites that align with your brand and that you feel comfortable with.

Today, the four main platforms that work best for independent estate agents are:

- Facebook

- Instagram

- LinkedIn

- Twitter

This list is in order of importance, although Instagram and LinkedIn are tied for second place if you're more comfortable on LinkedIn than Instagram. You don't have to post to all these platforms; I suggest you choose two. And if the BLAST Formula is completely alien to you, and if you would need time to implement it and get your team on board, then just start with Facebook and get used to posting from the formula every day. Only move on to a second platform once you feel confident you're getting results with Facebook. If you're deciding between LinkedIn and Instagram, let me ask you this: do you have a library of beautiful lifestyle images of houses you can post from? If so, Instagram is the best platform for you. If you feel that your property photographs aren't good enough to populate your Instagram feed, but you have great landlord content, then I suggest you use LinkedIn as your second platform. Even though each of these four platforms has its own culture, style and feel, my BLAST Formula will work just as well on each. Post consistently and frequently on any of them using the formula, and your likes, your followers and your connections will rise.

Email marketing

How to get your emails opened and read

- **A great subject line.** If your email doesn't have a compelling subject line, you won't get past the first hurdle. But don't be tempted to use a clickbait approach. I know marketers who use just the recipient's first name as the subject, or 'hi'. These tactics may get your email opened, but your response rate will be dismal and your unsubscribe rate higher as a consequence. People don't like feeling they've been tricked into taking an action.

  Get your subject line right and you're halfway there. Let me ask you this – which of these emails would you be most likely to open?

  - Three things you can do today to get more viewings

  - Company update: new Bromley branch opening this month

  - Connells' Summer newsletter

  If you answered #1, you're right. The other two are actual emails I've received but not opened. The first one is mine, and has a 46% open rate, which is pretty good.

- **Talk like a friend.** Don't go all formal and pretend to be a corporate. Be yourself. Use words you usually use in conversation, and make sure your emails have a natural voice that reflects your personality.

- **Give, don't request.** You're not writing to ask for a valuation. You're writing to give the reader something that will enhance and strengthen the relationship you have with them.

- **Ask simple questions.** You can ask a question, provided the answer is easy for the recipient to respond with. 'Tell me about your biggest selling challenge' or 'Why are you moving?' are questions that are too big and involved for them to answer on an email, so they won't yield the number of responses you may be hoping for. By contrast, 'Which of these two for-sale board designs do you like best?' is simple to answer, and you'll get many more responses from an email like this.

- **Add a PS.** It's a well-known sales letter tactic to add a PS, and that's because it works. People are busy, and they will often only read the first line and the PS. If these are compelling enough for them to go back for a second read, they'll scan to see if your email is relevant and interesting to them. Your PS could be the difference between getting a response and hearing crickets.

- **Add a photo of yourself.** There are a couple of reasons to add a photo of yourself at the bottom of your emails: 1) it's a personal touch that is likely to elicit a response from the recipient, and 2) it allows your email service provider to more accurately measure your email open rates.

So you don't feel overwhelmed and confused about the steps you need to take to get your email marketing working for you, I've created an actionable list of just five steps:

STEP 1 – Build your list. Focus on building a list of quality, motivated vendors and landlords. Use Facebook ads, social media, blogging, leaflets and any of your regular marketing channels to drive traffic to an email capture, rather than trying to skip steps by going straight for the valuation.

STEP 2 – Create a nurture sequence. Write a series of emails that are full of tips and advice, and stay away from trying to sell them anything, then set up an auto-mated schedule for sending them to save you time. By having your emails drip out at regular intervals, you'll make sure your email subscribers stay warm, interested and engaged.

STEP 3 – Keep your subscribers separate from your CRM. Don't try to use Vebra, Jupix, or whatever CRM you're using, to communicate and convert your email subscribers. Instead, use a dedicated email marketing service, like AWeber, Mailchimp or Infusionsoft; these are just three of the many that are available and that integrate easily with most third-party landing page software platforms.

STEP 4 – Mine your database regularly. Your existing database – that is, all your past vendors, landlords and applicants – can be a real treasure trove of new leads. Instead of cold-calling them all, and 'prospecting' to them, take a smarter approach: email them asking if they would like something of value, like an e-book, checklist or other informative piece of content. This content should not only tempt them to click to get it; it should also tell you something about them. For example, offering your entire database a checklist called '17 Steps You Need to Take Before You Put Your Home on the Market' means that anyone who chooses to download it is probably considering selling relatively soon. No need to segment your database: the checklist does the work for you.

STEP 5 – Encourage engagement at each step. The purpose of your email marketing is to provoke a response from the recipient. A response can lead to an email conversation, which in turn can lead to a phone conversation, and from there it's only a small step to be invited out. So, ask questions that have easy answers, offer multiple-choice questions, and ask for help and feedback. Any email that can generate a reply from someone on your list is working for you, so apply the formula to other emails. Just don't overdo it – you don't need a question in each email.

A word about GDPR

If you blast your CRM database with marketing messages, you're in breach of the GDPR regulations. After all, why would someone who viewed a property with you in 2009 be happy to get an email from you today, offering a free valuation? Instead, by using a reputable email marketing service provider, you'll stay within the rules by getting your subscriber's permission to send them useful tips and advice, by monitoring your open rates and complaint numbers, and by offering an unsubscribe option on every email.

What are you trying to achieve with your email marketing?

Your goal is to **capture** your audience's attention, **connect** with them by generating a response, and **convert** them into a valuation appointment – when it's appropriate and helpful for them to go to that next step.

The 'capture' part of the funnel is at the top, when your audience first comes into contact with your content. They may read some of your articles and blog posts, perhaps follow you on social media and watch a video. If they are still interested in what you have to say and the information you share, you need to offer them the next step of 'paying' for your next-level content with their email address. This requires them to place trust in you – no one these days gives up their email address lightly – and once you have the ability to email them, you need to make sure your content is worthy of their trust by sending them genuinely valuable information and useful updates. This is the 'connect' part of the funnel. 'Convert' is when they pick up the phone, reply to your email or send a message, and book a valuation with you.

Remember that this person could be enjoying your emails and content for years before they decide to take the next step with you, so be patient. People rarely decide to sell their homes overnight; it takes months and sometimes years of discussion and planning for them to get to that stage, and if you're communicating positively and helpfully with them during their decision period, it's much more likely you'll get the invite to value their home and win the final instruction.

Digital assets

A digital asset is any piece of content in digital form that you have created (proprietary content). If you offer the digital asset in return for contact information – eg, email address, phone number – it acts as a 'lead magnet', sometimes called a 'subscriber briber'. A digital asset can be a checklist, video tutorial, guide or anything you give away in exchange for someone's contact details.

Ideally, your digital asset sits on a 'landing page', which is simply a web page designed specifically to convert a visitor into a subscriber. Largely devoid of distracting information and links, the landing page gives a visitor only two choices: subscribe or leave.

It can be expensive getting your web developer to add landing pages to your website, particularly if you need to update them or add new ones often. It's better to use a dedicated third-party landing page tool like LeadPages or ClickFunnels, which are easy to use and bolt on to your website. You can even use them completely independently of your website, although bear in mind that the URLs (web addresses) tend to be long and wouldn't be ideal to use on print media (eg, a direct mail letter or printed advert).

The lead magnets that work best

It's tempting to write down everything you know about estate agency and create your own version of *War and Peace*, then offer it to everyone. But that's not the best strategy to create a lead magnet. Lead magnets work best when they are specific and therefore appeal to a small segment of your audience – preferably your ideal client. Instead of writing 'The Ultimate Guide to Selling Your Home', which is meant for everyone but far too broad to have strong appeal, try 'How to Plan for a Successful Downsize Move'. That way, anyone who clicks and downloads your guide will be interested in downsizing (or perhaps will pass it on to a parent or someone else who is). I know you can probably write tens of thousands of words on the subject of planning a successful downsize move, but the best lead magnets are fairly short and quick to consume. You don't want someone to spend the next few months wading through your content before they finally get in contact with you. If they're impressed by your content and you can give them an early 'win' by downloading it and taking immediate action, you're much more likely to get a phone call or enquiry from them within twenty-four to seventy-two hours.

How to create your lead magnet

Once you've planned your lead magnet and written your text, you need to make it look attractive and brand it. You can either used a graphic designer or try doing it yourself. I find PowerPoint to be an easy way to create a professional-looking guide or checklist. Once your content is attractive and branded, you can simply convert it to a PDF and upload it to whichever platform you're using to deliver it.

Instant valuation tool funnel

This strategy is a little bit more advanced than the others, but if you've got your direct mail, content and social media all sorted, a Facebook Ad funnel is a good place to turn your attention to next. Most instant online valuation tools will work for this funnel.

Let's run through these steps, one at a time:

Step 1 – Add the Facebook pixel to your website

The Facebook pixel is just a little piece of code that you or your web developer can insert into the 'back end' of your website. It's a tracker that allows Facebook to identify which of its users have been to your website, and then it allows you to serve up an advert to them on Facebook. You're probably familiar with the concept of browsing, say, a sofa on the John Lewis website, then that sofa 'following' you around the internet for weeks. It's the same idea with Facebook. With a pixeled site, you can show a website visitor an advert based on what pages they've been to on your website. Clever, isn't it?

To create your Facebook pixel, just go to your Facebook Ads Manager and under the 'Measure and Report' menu heading, you'll find 'Events Manager' and 'Pixels'. In here, Facebook takes you through the steps you need to take to create and set up your pixel, including inviting you to email the pixel, together with instructions, straight to your web developer.

Step 2 – Create your Facebook Audience

Once you have your pixel installed correctly on your website, you can set up a Facebook Audience. Just go to the Ads Manager and click on the 'Audience' menu heading. Click the big blue button named 'Create Audience' and choose 'Custom Audience'. In the 'Sources' menu, choose 'Website Traffic'.

From here, choose the longest time frame available, which is currently 180 days, and name your audience something like 'Home Styling Blog Post' plus the date. Facebook will then generate a list of its users who have visited your blog post in the last 180 days and create an audience from this list. Although you don't get to see who is on this list, Facebook will invite you to create an advert for them, which we'll do in Step 3 below.

Step 3 – Create an advert for this audience

You can create an advert to show to this new audience you've generated by clicking on the big green 'Create an ad' button in the Facebook Ads Manager dashboard. Under 'Audience', start typing the name of your new audience – eg, 'Home Styling Blog Post' – and it should pop up as a targeting option. Select it, and add your audience age range (we usually use ages thirty to sixty) and the geographical area you cover (perhaps your office location plus a 20-mile radius). A word of warning: don't add any interests here whatsoever – your audience will reduce to a tiny size and Facebook won't show your advert in the newsfeed.

Now you've targeted the right people, let's move on to Step 4.

Step 4 – Take them to an instant valuation tool

Once you've chosen your audience and set up your budget and schedule, it's time to create the advert itself. We call this the 'creative', which, in simple terms, is the image and text. I'm not going to go into too much detail here about ad creative strategy, or this step will end up being eighty pages long! But here are some guidelines you'll find helpful if you're doing this for the first time or if you'd like to improve the results you're currently getting:

- ✔ Use the same image in your ad that you've used as the background to your ValPal page. Facebook likes congruence, and so do its users – especially if they've never heard of you before.

- ✔ Be specific in your copy. We've found that using phrases like, 'In just 57 seconds' gets more clicks than if you just write, 'Find out now'.

- ✔ Experiment with using the 'call to action' button and with ads that don't have any button at all. We find that no button wins over using, say, 'Learn more', but only marginally. Test it for yourself to see what works best with your audience.

- ✔ If your audience is small (less than 2,000 people), don't run your ad for any longer than a week at a time or you'll 'exhaust' your audience.

Make sure you pixel your ValPal page, too, so you can retarget anyone who visits the page and who doesn't complete the form. You can even target someone who did complete the form, with a blog post or article about when to book a valuation. Be creative with your thinking and put yourself in your audience's shoes – what would they want to read next after taking each action?

Connecting your lead magnet to your digital marketing funnel

You'll need to make sure that whenever anyone downloads your free lead magnet their contact details are captured and fed into whatever email marketing software you're using. In simple terms, when someone types in their name and email address and clicks 'Submit', not only do they need to receive the promised guide or checklist, their name and email address also need to be automatically added to your database so you can email them in the future. That's why it's usually simpler, and in the long run more cost-effective, to use third-party tools to create your landing pages. That way, you can turn your lead magnet into a digital marketing funnel without ever needing to pay your web developer big sums to try to create a custom solution – off-the-shelf is far easier for you to create and administer.

Paid traffic

To make sure new people are shown your lead magnet and join your subscriber base, you'll also need to use paid traffic. Facebook, Google, Twitter, LinkedIn and Instagram all offer an advertising platform to small businesses like yours that want to grow their audience. Most are easy to use, but they're also easy to waste money on while you figure out what actually works. I had a client who ended up spending £35 per subscriber while he was experimenting with Facebook Ads; and, given that he couldn't afford to continue with his experiment, he never did discover how to use Facebook Ads to get downloads and therefore subscribers. While it would take a whole book to explore all the nuances of paid traffic (and it would be out of date before it left the printer's), there are some basic principles that are true of most online advertising platforms and that should stand the test of time:

1. Find out what works organically before putting ad spend behind it. If your free checklist isn't getting traction on your Facebook page or Twitter feed, it's not going to be more popular as an advert.

2. Keep your advert benefit focused. Most people won't care if they see an advert for the 'Downton's Estate Agent's Guide to Moving House', but if they spot an ad that promises the '10 Secrets to a Quick House Sale' they're much more likely to click on it.

3. Use a variety of different audiences. Just using 'cold' audiences – where you simply select the geographical area and perhaps the age range and interests of the people you want to target – will prove expensive and may be viewed as low relevance by the social platform you're using. If you combine cold audiences with targeting those followers you already have, you'll find your adverts are much more effective. A 'warm' audience can be someone who has been to your

website (called a 'retargeting' or 'remarketing' audience) or who is already following and engaging with your social content.

4. Test lots of different visuals. We find that photos of houses don't tend to get as much interest as more 'lifestyle' images – for example, a dog on an armchair – or even a completely random image like colourful balloons. When setting up your campaigns, test at least three different images to see what works best to attract your audience. You may be surprised at the results – I always am.

5. When testing your adverts, only test one element at a time. For example, if you change the image to see which one works best for you (see point 4 above), don't change the text, too, or you won't know which change altered the results. Always change only one element at once, keeping all the other elements the same, so you can measure and compare accurately.

If you'd like to know more about how we could help you with your digital marketing funnels, go to http://bit.ly/bookacallwithsam and book a call with me.

SIX

Converting High Value Homes

Where are your valuations coming from?

I've found conclusively that the chances of winning the instruction are directly correlated with the source of the valuation. For example, if you've been invited to a house simply because the owner has seen your for-sale boards, there's a pretty low chance of you winning that instruction. If, however, the vendor received a letter from you, one that was well-written, using language in alignment with your core values, and that included a photo of you, you have a much higher chance of converting that valuation to an instruction.

Many independent agents have a hard time coming to terms with this principle. They want to believe that the market appraisals that come in via 'word of mouth', which tends to be a combination of brand awareness and referral or recommendation, are the strongest leads that are most likely to convert. But, in my experience, this is not the case. To add insult to injury, I've found that not only do you have less chance of winning the instruction, these vendors are more disposed to negotiate hard on fee.

Marketing is the answer to this problem. Effective marketing will ensure that your leads come to you from targeted sources – from vendors who have been educated via your content, meaning they understand and appreciate your differentiators and what you stand for. They have asked you to value their home *because* of your marketing efforts, not in spite of them, so they are much warmer, less resistant to your fee, and far more inclined to value you and your team. In short, the leads you create generate better clients.

Preparing for your market appraisal

While it's important to prepare for each valuation visit, take care not to put too much store in the data. Yes, it's handy to know that next door sold for £50,000 over the asking price in just a week, but if you focus on the numbers you may miss paying close attention to the human aspect of the valuation – the clients. Their needs, wants, wishes and dreams are much more important to understand than the fact there's a house on the same road that hasn't sold for a year.

There is valuable data in Rightmove and the other portals, of course – particularly data related to the people who you are going to see. You can't see the mitigating factor behind the house that hasn't sold in a year (smelly dogs, grumpy vendor, unhygienic teen), but you can see whether your prospective client has tried to sell their house before, and for how much.

You can also calculate the price per square foot of comparable properties, which, if you're going to see a unique home, can be invaluable information. I've lost count of the instructions we've won on the vendor's delight at our 'scientific' valuation process. To conduct your own square foot analysis, go to your favoured portal and set a search parameter that makes sense for the house in question. Look for the total floor area, which could be on the floorplan, on the pdf brochure or in the Energy Performance Certificate (EPC) (you may need to look up the EPC on the official site). Choose either metric or imperial to record your data in, and add the data to a spreadsheet. If the total square footage includes any outbuildings or a detached garage, exclude this figure from the total. We include attached garages, so long as they are properly built, and not just a lean-to or a car port. You'll need around fifteen to twenty comparable properties for the data to be useful; then, if you're using Excel, you can calculate the average with the click of a button. If the house you're going to see isn't yet on the market, and hasn't been recently, there may be no record of a total floor area, so you'll have to use your best guesstimate once you're in the market appraisal. We're pretty good at guesstimating now, but it does take some practice. Try thinking of a home you're already marketing that is similar in size and working from that.

What to take to your market appraisal

Many agents are surprised when we tell them we don't take any marketing materials to our market appraisals, nor do we take a Rightmove Best Price Guide. All we take is a selection of our current brochures. That way, we make sure we stay focused on them and what we can do for them when it comes to marketing their home. Take along a corporate brochure and you'll be tempted to talk about you and your agency. And anyway, it'll only end up in a pile of everyone else's brochures, then eventually in the recycling bin. Save yourself the time, effort and expense, and avoid those corporate brochures that agents love. They're just not worth it. If you want to prove you're different, don't do what everyone else does. Take a different path.

What to wear on your market appraisal

Image is everything, and the moment that client opens their door to you they make a snap judgement about who you are, and even about your values, by the way you look. It may not be fair, but it's true.

Take the case of an agent who turns up late, rushing and arriving flustered on the vendor's doorstep. He's wearing a cheap suit that could do with a dry clean, a shirt that isn't quite as white as it once was and a garish tie his mum gave him three Christmases ago. Looking down, his shoes haven't been polished in a while and his hair could do with a cut. Oh, and he's hoping the stubble he's sporting will be viewed as trendy, not as evidence that he didn't have (make) time to shave this morning. Get the picture?

Now be unkind, and let's make some judgements about him:

- He's lazy

- He's disorganised

- He's not very successful

- He doesn't take a personal pride in his appearance

- He has an 'it'll do' attitude

Disagree with any of the above?

Now let's imagine that one of my wonderful team rings the doorbell, exactly on time. She is calm because she arrived a few minutes early and parked around the corner to prep for her visit. She is dressed smartly, not in a suit but wearing a good-quality jacket, and her shoes are polished. Her hair is clean and shiny, and her make-up subtle. The overall impression is of someone well-groomed. She greets her client with a big smile and shakes their hand warmly.

What assumptions do you make about her? How about:

- She's conscientious

- She's well-organised

- She's efficient

- She's professional and successful

- She wants to make a good impression

You will be judged instantly on the doorstep. The vendor or landlord may even make an irreversible decision about whether or not to instruct you, in that moment. I'm not suggesting that you wear a suit (we don't), but adhere to whatever dress code you have and encourage your team to take pride in their appearances by making sure you do, too.

How to follow up

We hear over and over again, 'The money is in the follow-up', but how do you tread that fine line between hassling someone with too many phone calls and losing the instruction to a competitor because you didn't follow up enough?

One change I'd like to encourage you to make is to stop thinking about the frequency of your follow-up, and instead turn your attention to the method.

Have you ever made a video for a prospective client? The chances are that your answer is 'no', because rarely have I heard of any agent doing so. But it's what we do. We say we're different from any other agent, so we have to be different – which means acting differently. And one of the ways in which we do this is by creating a video as a follow-up for some of the clients we visit.

There are usually specific reasons for us to create a video for a client we've seen for a market appraisal. Perhaps one of the decision makers couldn't be present, or it's an instruction we know we have strong competition for. By creating a video explaining what we do, or reiterating our thoughts and recommendations, we are not only creating something very memorable for the client; we are also proving our claim that we are, indeed, different.

Aside from the video, when I get asked how many times you need to follow up, my answer is simple: 'as many times as it takes'. There is no point in stopping until you get the instruction; but to make sure you're not hassling the client, on each follow-up call simply agree the date you will next phone them. A vendor who is expecting a call from you in the next few days or weeks is unlikely to give the instruction to another agent without calling you beforehand.

Other ways to follow up are with a handwritten note, a small gift (perhaps something seasonal like an Easter egg), or a brochure of a home you've recently taken to the market or sold. Just make sure that you're not doing what every other agent is doing, or else you'll get what every other agent will get.

Become a converting LEGEND

Converting high value homes from valuation to instruction is a skill you need to develop, if you haven't already. To help you become more successful at converting, I've developed a formula which we use on every valuation we go to. We convert at 90% and higher, winning almost every instruction we want – a success rate we attribute to this powerful formula that I call LEGEND:

Listen

Explore

Gap

Educate

Needs

Decision

Not only have we been using this formula for over fifteen years, I've also taught it to countless clients, who have used it to win high value instructions in their area. Once you learn it, understand it and practice implementing it, you too will be winning the instructions you want most and leave your competitors wondering what happened.

Before we dive in, you'll notice that we don't begin the market appraisal with the house tour – that comes much later. You'll see why once we reach that point in the meeting. But for now, let's look at the first section in the formula:

Listen

You may think you know how to listen. I thought I did, too, until I heard this anecdotal quote:

'Listening is not just waiting to speak'.

I realised that's exactly what I was doing: waiting to speak. So, I stopped doing it. It wasn't an easy habit to break, and it's something I still find hard, even now. But when I listen – truly listen – with no plan of what I'm going to say in response, I hear those cues and clues I would otherwise have missed. Often, the vendor isn't saying what's truly on their mind and is only sharing surface information. By listening properly, you will pick up on the information just under the surface that will give you insights into their motivations and concerns, and that help you to serve them more fully.

Every vendor has a story to tell. They want to tell you why they're selling, or why they've tried to sell and failed, or even why they don't want to sell right now. Nobody reaches the decision to move overnight. Often, the larger the home, the longer it takes somebody to decide to sell it. That may be because the house has been in the family for generations or because the owners are considering downsizing after many years. The story of how they came to their decision to move, all the determining factors surrounding their plans and their anxieties over what could go wrong – they will usually share all this information and more, if you just give them the space and time to tell you their story.

Listening properly and being genuinely interested makes people feel important. Telling them about your agency, and how long you've been in business, doesn't.

> People will forget what you said, people will forget what you did, but people will never forget how you made them feel.
> — Maya Angelou

Explore

Although you need to know why the vendors are moving, it's important that you are careful about asking them. Just asking, 'Why are you moving?' may elicit an emotional response, or a defensive one. There are easier questions to ask that can tell you all you need to know, like 'How long have you lived here?' or 'Tell me about your moving plans?' – both of which will often reveal their motivations and thoughts.

As you uncover the real reasons behind their moving plans, you need to sensitively delve into each one in more detail. For example, if it's an older person, perhaps they're moving because the house is now too big for them. But what are the consequences of living in too large a home? Worry about the garden? Difficulties using the stairs? Anxiety about the maintenance and running costs? Discovering how their current home is affecting them in a negative way is all part of being able to expertly guide and advise your clients, whatever they choose to do.

If the move is a discretionary one, as opposed to compulsory, this may affect your valuation and the timescale of the sale, which you'll need to bear in mind when you come to the 'educate' part of the valuation. That's why uncovering not only the surface information but also the hidden motivators and concerns is vital at this stage. Just be sensitive and aware that the insights you reveal may be charged with emotion and be difficult for you both to deal with.

Gap

The 'gap' of the LEGEND formula is the space or journey between where the vendors are now and where they want to be. For example, 'where they are now' could be in a house that's too small for them, and that is causing stress and discomfort, and 'where they want to be is' in a larger home, with more space and additional rooms, so that they feel more free and able to lead the lifestyle they want. The more difficult their current situation and the more desirable their future state, the bigger the gap. Too small a gap equals low motivation. A very big gap will always make for a more motivated seller.

It's your job to highlight the gap your client is facing right now, so that they appreciate the potential pitfalls of staying where they are. The better you can paint a picture for them of their future life, the more motivated they will be to reach it. We often talk to vendors who have become despondent about their house sale, doubting they will ever be able to move into their ideal home. We help them see, through careful questioning, that what they want is achievable, and we paint a picture of the journey we will take together to get them there. It's empowering for you and for them when you get this part right.

Remember that the topic of conversation in a market appraisal is the person sitting in front of you, not you and your agency. Be clear about your role in this very important decision they are facing, and the responsibility you are offering to take on. As estate agents, we can change people's lives, forever. It's a huge responsibility and, done right, hugely rewarding. But never forget the duty you have to your clients to help them make the right decisions that will give them the outcomes they truly want.

Before you move onto the 'Educate' section of LEGEND, it's time to look around the house. There are several reasons why you need to do the house tour now, rather than earlier:

1. It gives you the chance to build up rapport before you look around the house, so you can ask more questions as you look.

2. It makes sure you put the spotlight firmly on them, and not their house, in the first part of the market appraisal.

3. It lets you make comments and suggestions about the way in which they're presenting their home, once you've built up trust in the 'listen', 'explore' and 'gap' sections of the visit.

4. It makes for a natural break in the valuation visit, which gives everyone the chance to digest the information discussed and ask appropriate questions.

5. Asking them difficult questions when you're not sitting facing them can be more sensitive and can make it easier for them to answer honestly.

Educate

Once you sit back down, it's time for the 'educate' part of the LEGEND formula. This is not the time for you to pitch or to tell the vendor everything you've ever learned about estate agency. Whatever you tell them at this point needs to be entirely relevant to the information and insights you've gathered so far on your visit. A good question to ask the vendor here, to make sure you're on track with the information you need to tell them, is: 'What made you call us out?' If they talk about your photography or brochures, you know you need to focus on how you'll market their home visually and tangibly. If, however, they say it's because you sold a neighbour's house, or that you seem to sell homes of the same calibre as theirs, then instead concentrate on case studies and what you've already sold nearby. By keeping your feedback and information entirely relevant to them and exactly what they're looking for in an agent, you'll ensure you hold their attention in this section.

A great way to make sure you cover all the points you need to, without waffling, is to use the 'feedback sandwich' method. The three elements you need to include in your advice are: presentation, price and promotion, and I'd suggest tackling them in that order.

Presentation – This is how their home is currently presented, whether it's ready for photography and viewings, and if they need to change anything to prepare it.

Price – This goes in the middle of your feedback sandwich to make sure you don't put too much emphasis on it. Price is only one element of the saleability of a house, and if you place too much importance on it you risk losing the instruction to a competitor who values the home higher. If the home is unique and tricky to value, don't feel you have to give a valuation there and then. Better to wait until you've had chance to think it over. I've been caught out before by how much I've loved a particular aspect of the house, or even how nice the vendors are, which has skewed my valuation upwards, but then, on reflection, I realised I'd over-valued the house, which doesn't serve anyone. Give yourself the chance to consider all the various factors, and do your research, so you are confident about the valuation you give (upon which you will be judged).

Promotion – This is where you describe how you will market your client's home. It's a crucial part of the market appraisal because it moves a client from thinking like an interviewer – usually interviewing three prospective 'candidates' before deciding on who to give the instruction to – to thinking more like a vendor, imagining their home in print and on Rightmove, and getting viewings. Psychologically, this is a powerful motivator for them to choose you – the agent who enabled them to think like a seller.

Needs

We're almost at the end of the market appraisal, so it's time to wrap up. The 'needs' section is where you'll clarify what the vendor has already told you – importantly, in their own words – to demonstrate and reassure them that you have listened and understood their situation. By doing this, you'll also discover anything you've misunderstood or have forgotten to ask. For example, if you ask, 'I know you've found your dream home; can I just check, can you buy that home without selling this house?' the answer they give you may change the advice you give them and the sale strategy you recommend. It's important you've asked all the right questions, and this section lets you check that you've understood their situation correctly.

In any given house move, there are three factors at play: time, effort and money. Every vendor places a different weight on each, and you need to be confident you've understood their priorities. An older woman downsizing into a sheltered housing unit may be far more worried about moving her late husband's possessions than she is about the time it will take to sell her home or the value she'll realise from the sale. By contrast, a young upsizing family will place a higher emphasis on the timescale, especially if they have a job move or school term dates to fit around.

By reiterating their situation as you've understood it, both you and the vendor will be more confident you have all the facts.

Decision

The final part of LEGEND is the decision. This is one of the most important parts of the whole formula, yet it's the part most agents forget to include in their market appraisal process. I'm going to share with you how to make sure you leave the valuation with a clear agreement on what will happen next, and how to significantly reduce the number of pending decisions you get.

If you follow my formula, you'll use the word 'decision' three times, in three questions. Here's how it looks in practice:

Question 1 – Have you made a decision? This first question is to ascertain if the vendor is actually ready to instruct you and go ahead. Don't leave this question unasked – you risk losing an instruction you already had in the bag but didn't know it.

Question 2 – It's _____ day today; would _____ days give you enough time to make a decision? Depending on their situation, which you've appraised and understood over the last hour or more, give them a couple of days, or longer. Often, including a weekend gives them a reassuring time period and helps them relax.

Question 3 – OK, I'll call you on _____ [day] at _____ [time] for your decision, is that right? Now they are expecting to give you their decision on the given day and at a specific time. Everyone's clear about what's going to happen next, and you'll avoid calling several times to ask bland questions and worry about the alternate risks of hassling them or losing the instruction to a competitor.

This process helps make sure you get to a quick decision in the majority of cases, and it also makes sure you are in control of the market appraisal throughout, which in turn helps you appear more confident and professional.

Price your service based on your worth

What's it worth for someone to be able to move on with their life? To get out of debt? To cut their commute? To spend more time with their family? To live in a home that fits them perfectly? When you are great at what you do, you should be commanding a premium price. You deserve to be paid the best, because you deliver the best. Setting your fee this way sends a signal to potential clients that you're not going to waste their time and that only you have the solution they've been longing for.

People want to work with the best. It tells them that they are in the right place. If clients came to you ready to take your advice and eager to pay the premium price for your services, because your positioning was clear and powerful, how much faster would you hit your income goals?

I was recently chatting to a young valuations manager who told me he wasn't getting into the high value homes in his area. At the time of our conversation, his highest property listed was £390,000, although he did have seventy-five properties listed, which is higher than the average office has.

I asked what he would charge, if he did manage to get through the door of a £1 million property. Here's what he said, word-for-word:

'I'll quote 1%, but if I'm up against other agents I'll drop to 0.75% or even 0.5%.'

When I asked him if he thought a high value home-owner would be put off by such a low fee, he didn't understand the question.

I then asked him what he would say to the vendor of a high value home, if he had the opportunity of a market appraisal. Here's what he said:

'I'd tell them which portals we use, including premium listings, and tell them about the company.'

What about photography and brochures, I asked him?

'We can do photography ourselves which we are happy with, and nobody looks at brochures, so we just have them on our website.'

If the owner of a high value home chose to use this person's agency, they would be motivated by one differentiator only: the fact that he was the cheapest. Nothing he was offering was different from any other agent in his area. And the problem with being the cheapest is that someone else can always offer even cheaper fees. In fact, I recently talked to a new agent who wants to offer the cheapest fees in the UK: £99. Ignoring the flawed thinking that has gone into this idea, if you could only be either the cheapest or the best, which would you choose?

You see, for you to charge the fees you want to charge, you have to be worth it. If you're charging what everyone else is charging and offering what every other agent is offering, you're simply a commodity. And you can't blame a vendor for choosing a commodity agent based on price. Leave those vendors to Purplebricks and the onlines – they are not your clients.

High fees are your reward for having a differentiated service

How do you attract the best clients? Simple: with the best marketing materials. When you think of prestige property marketing, which agents come to mind?

Fifteen years ago, Savills, Knight Frank, and Fine & Country were agents at the cutting edge of luxury property marketing and leading the way for the rest of us. Now the property marketing landscape has changed.

What was cutting edge is now the new normal; what was considered innovative is now standard.

To truly stand out in the ways that matter to your dream homeowners, you need to take your property marketing to a whole new level. You can't charge top fees and then deliver only a mediocre service. Owners of large, luxury homes expect a sophisticated suite of marketing services. Professional photography is no longer enough to impress these high value homeowners; you need to give them beautiful lifestyle images of their elegantly styled homes. Unique and exclusive homes need unique and exclusive marketing. Offer this, and you, too, can attract the homes you most want to list and sell.

Your true worth

Picasso was enjoying a double espresso in his favourite café in Paris one day, when he was accosted by a woman at a nearby table.

'*Excusez-moi*, aren't you Picasso?' she asked excitedly. When he confirmed that he was, she begged him to draw her portrait. With a sigh, he took a clean napkin off the table and a pencil out of his pocket, and quickly drew the woman's likeness. As he passed the napkin to the woman, he asked her for 500 francs.

'But,' she spluttered, 'it only took you a minute!'

'*Non, madame,*' Picasso explained. 'It took me forty years.'

This nice little story is probably apocryphal but illustrates something important: your worth. When a vendor complains that you've sold their property in two days for the full asking price, and therefore shouldn't be entitled to your full fee because all you did was put it on Rightmove, they are missing the point. (Several points, in fact.) You sold it quickly because you're excellent at what you do. You could have messed up the online advert, taken a load of unflattering photographs, made a hash of the description, and put any potential buyers off – if not on the phone, then on the viewing itself.

You did none of these things. Firstly, you chose to pay a hefty subscription to Rightmove in the first place. That's not a small undertaking by any means. Then, you worked hard to make sure your client's home looked as appealing as possible online, attracting interest from the right kind of buyers. You then negotiated a great offer and did everything in your power to make sure it stuck.

Not only that, but you pay thousands of pounds every month to make sure your office is professional and inviting and your staff are carefully-chosen and well-trained. You have even invested in clever software that allows you to spend less time on the less important stuff and more time actually helping your clients.

I'm guessing, too, that you work much more than a thirty-nine-hour week, that – if you're the boss – your hourly rate is less than that of your top salespeople, and that you check and answer emails from home, at weekends and probably on holiday, too. So, before you allow your fee to be questioned, whether on a market appraisal or after an accepted offer, remember this: you did not become a great agent overnight. You work hard, and you deserve to be paid what you're worth.

The Experience Age of estate agency

The Experience Age of estate agency is now upon us. What I've seen over the last ten years is a steady polarisation in the industry: a pull to one side of the market or the other. Homeowners looking to sell are either attracted to the cost-saving DIY agents or else they feel they need a high-touch, full-service agent to sell their home better. The middle-market agents are, frankly, doomed.

Think about the middle market in terms of retail. Remember Woolworths? Apart from the 'pick and mix' counter (I loved those strawberry creams), they weren't known for selling anything specific, and that was ultimately their downfall. Same with BHS and Dixons; these were all big brands in their time, but without a focus, something they were known for, they couldn't survive. It's the same with jewellery. If you wanted to buy a gold-plated bracelet for less than £20, chances are you'd head for Argos or H. Samuel. But if you're looking for a special anniversary gift for the love of your life, you're more likely to consider Tiffany or De Beers – both brands that would allow you to make a statement to the recipient that they are important to you. Just by examining our own buying habits, we can see that mediocre, middle-market brands are disappearing. People either want to buy on price or they want an experience.

Most independent agents will not embrace this new Experience Age. This is a crucial time in estate agency, so if you want to thrive, not just survive, and not be another statistic of failure (150 agents last year went bankrupt), it's time to make a change. When you change your strategy and stop being an agent for everyone, you need to give the highest levels of experience to your clients by focusing on the things that matter to them.

You're going to become all the things that a high value client needs the most: a personal adviser, a hand-holder, a voice of reason and experience, a mentor and, if appropriate, a friend. The more of these roles you can serve for your clients, the higher your value will be to them. These justify your fee and motivate high value referrals, too.

Not every client needs a full-service agent

There are some homeowners who are digitally accomplished and social savvy, who can take their own photos, upload them and write a decent description. These homeowners may own a standard home, understand how to present it for sale and are capable of doing their own viewings. All these homeowners need from an estate agent is to be listed on the portals. It would be very difficult to persuade them that your unique offering will justify a higher fee than an online agent would charge, and they certainly wouldn't pay upwards of 1.5%. And they are probably right.

Let me give you a metaphor to illustrate this concept. Imagine that you are about to go on holiday, flying out early in the morning. You decide to book a hotel room for the night before, for you and your family, so you avoid stresses in the morning. You compare two hotels: the Premier Inn and the Radisson Blu. The Premier Inn is a two-star hotel costing £80 a night. It's a bus ride away from the airport, offers a buffet breakfast and has a refreshments machine in the lobby. The Radisson Blu, on the other hand, is right in the terminal building. It's got a beautiful à la carte breakfast, a mini bar, a pool and a gym. But it costs £180 a night.

Which would you choose? Chances are you'd book the Premier Inn, for one simple reason: because none of us wants to pay for extra services we don't need. If all you need is a clean room for the night so you can get to the airport without fuss, there's no point in paying extra for a hotel that has a pool and a gym.

That's why the Premier Inn is the right choice. And the Radisson Blu doesn't want you either because you don't value the service and the experience that they offer. They want clients who appreciate their service and understand the value of it, just like you want to attract clients who are prepared to pay for a high quality of service and a special experience.

Those sellers who don't want those services – and, frankly, don't need them – are not your clients. Leave them to the DIY agents. Stop trying to compete for them. And whatever you do, *do not offer a full service for an online fee*. Imagine the Radisson Blu charging the same as the Premier Inn but offering a much higher level of service. Doing so would be a commercial disaster.

If you focus your time, energy and marketing on attracting your true clients – those who recognise the value of your service and experience and are happy to pay for them – and help them to reach their goals, they will love you for it. And of course, by focusing on your ideal clients, you don't need as many of them to be financially successful. Which would take the most resources to deliver, selling thirty houses at a £2,000 fee or just five houses at a £15,000 fee? They both reap the same revenue (£60,000), but selling thirty houses in the same timeframe as five needs a bigger staff to deliver more viewings and progress all those sales.

Agents often tell me they're worried that high value homes take longer to sell, but that's not always the truth. In fact, we recently sold a home with a £24,000 fee in just a week. And these quick sellers make up for the ones that do take longer to sell. Ultimately, it's going to come down to the fact that you need houses to sell houses. If you sell approximately 20% of your stock each month or so, then to sell one you'll need to have five listed, but to sell four you need to have twenty listed. At the time of writing, we have around thirty homes listed; twenty of those are over £700,000, and we're selling around six each month. With an average fee of over £10,000, we don't need to sell many to keep the bank manager (and ourselves) happy and continue serving our clients at the highest possible level.

If you'd like to know more about how we could help you install and implement the PROFIT Pyramid™ in your agency, go to http://bit.ly/bookacallwithsam and book a call with me.

SEVEN

Building Success Habits

Information without implementation has no value. It's what you do with what you've learned in this book that will set you apart from your competition and take your agency to a whole new level.

In this chapter, I'll share with you what I've found to be the vital components of a successful implementation plan. We'll start with my top focus and productivity tips, then look at the best KPIs (key performance indicators) to track for maximum results, moving on to creating your 90-Day Implementation Plan and, finally, exploring what a longer-term plan for your agency might look like.

This chapter is probably the most important one in this book. Why? Because without implementing the strategies and tactics in this book, what have you truly achieved?

First, let's look at why planning your marketing is so important. What you need to avoid at all costs is...

The 'feast and famine' cycle

I had this conversation with a Wiltshire agent recently:

Me: 'What marketing is working for you?'

Wiltshire: 'Canvassing, mainly. We send out 25,000 at a time and that usually gets us a phone call or two.'

Me: 'What's your canvassing plan?'

Wiltshire: 'We just send out a big batch when we're short of stock.'

Can you see the problem? This is how most agents market themselves: they have a big marketing push, expend lots of time, effort and money, and it works: the phone rings with a couple of nice instructions, so they stop marketing while they take those houses on. Once the flurry of activity has come to an end and they have time to catch their breath, they realise they have no more valuation appointments in the diary, so the marketing push starts all over again.

Is this you? If so, you're not alone. It's a common problem, especially among independent estate agents with small teams and no corporate marketing departments to back them up. This leads to a lack of marketing momentum which, in turn, leads to a lack of consistent leads and valuations. The problem with this style of marketing is that you're constantly in 'launch' mode, instead of having a 'lead generation machine' working in the background for you 24/7, bringing you enquiries even when you sleep.

The solution to the feast and famine cycle is a system. A marketing system means that your marketing happens *no matter what you, personally, are doing.* Many agents make the mistake of thinking that marketing is a creative role, but it isn't. In the main, it's much more of an administrative role. Administrators get things done; creatives dither. (As one of the latter, and a confirmed ditherer, I feel qualified to make this statement.)

I promise you, it's not more ideas you need in your agency, it's more implementation. The success or failure of your marketing is not based on the extent of your creativity. It's based on your ability to implement a plan, pure and simple.

Your marketing priorities

Here's your opportunity to get your marketing priorities straightened out. Most independent agents I speak to tell me that they have no idea what activities to spend their time on, and they end up spending way too much time on the wrong things – those things that are not going to make the boat go faster.

The PROFIT Pyramid™ consists of three fundamental marketing channels:

1. Direct Mail

2. Content

3. Funnels

These channels represent your most important marketing tasks. Without them, your other marketing activities will have to work so much harder – and so will you. Other marketing activities, like competitions, sponsorship and print advertising, will drain your limited time and marketing budget, so don't spread your focus too thinly. Stick to the PROFIT Pyramid™

until it's running like clockwork before you turn your attention to any additional marketing channels.

Getting your marketing priorities right and creating a marketing plan for implementation are both crucial elements of business growth; done right, they will help you stay in 'feast' and out of the clutches of 'famine', now and forevermore.

Now you know your marketing priorities, let's dive into planning.

Create your 90-Day Implementation Plan

Any marketing plan needs to contain these three basic elements:

1. Activity

2. Responsibility

3. Time

I find it best to put these into a spreadsheet, but you could use a Word document or even a whiteboard. For example, it could look like this:

Your 90 Day Implementation Plan

Activity	Responsibility	By when?
Direct mail letters x 100	Susie	Weekly

And if you're following my PROFIT Pyramid™, your marketing plan might look something like this:

Your 90 Day Implementation Plan

Activity type	Activity	Responsibility	By when?
DIRECT MAIL	Direct mail letters x 100	Susie	Weekly
CONTENT	Write blog post on top tips to sell quickly	David	End of month
FUNNELS	Write checklist for downsizers	Susie	End of month

As you can see, by adding a specific task and assigning that task to an individual with an expected delivery date, the plan looks much more doable. You've taken the task of marketing off the easel of 'creativity' and slammed it firmly onto the table of 'implementation'.

Your KPIs

A key performance indicator is measurable value that demonstrates how effectively a company is achieving its key business objectives. 'What gets inspected gets respected, and what gets measured can be improved',[4] says Captain Trevor Greene, Peace Warrior. And he's

---

4   Levinson, J. C and Gibson, S (2010) *Guerilla Social Media Marketing: 100+ Weapons to Grow Your Online Influence, Attract Customers, and Drive Profits.* Entrepreneur Press

right. As soon as you start measuring certain numbers in your business, you'll find they tend to start improving; and even if they don't, you become more aware of them and you can work on them more effectively.

What to track and how to track it

We keep our KPIs in a document we call a 'Scorecard'. Here's what we track:

Your 90 Day Implementation Plan

PERFORMANCE
Valuations
Instructions
Sold (including STC)
Current Stock

RESULTS
Completed
Banked
Banked year to date

AUDIENCE
Socials
Subscribers – Facebook Messenger
Subscribers – Email list
Website unique visitors

There are many numbers you could measure, but we have focused on the ones that make most difference to the performance – and therefore, growth – of our business. Plus, we only include those elements we can actually influence. We don't include viewings in our list of KPIs because they are nearly impossible to increase, and trying to increase them – via prospecting, for example – may harm the relationships we have with our buyers. The KPIs you choose to measure and monitor are personal to you and to your business growth plans. Choose them wisely, and don't be afraid to make changes as you need to.

We bring the Scorecard to our weekly meetings and share the results with our team. We took the decision early on to be transparent about all our metrics, including financial ones, so we share our banked figure each week, and also our year to date, and measure them against our financial goals. I think visual displays are strong motivators, so we also have what I call our 'church roof fund' chart in our kitchen, and we colour in squares each time we reach another £10,000 in the bank. Whether or not you're transparent on all financial aspects is at your discretion. For us, it fosters loyalty and trust in our team, and it emphasises the fact that our successes are the result of team effort.

Download your KPI Scorecard here: www.samashdown.co.uk/theselectiveagentbook.

Your longer-term growth plan for your agency

How long-term should you plan for your agency growth? In my experience, anything over three to six months will be a total guess, but having a big number in your mind will make you reach higher and further than if you don't.

We plan out our marketing activities three months in advance, but we know the goal we are aiming to reach over the next year, three years and five years. I also have personal ten-year goals but trying to forecast what your agency will look like a decade from now is probably best left to a fortune teller. (If you find a good one, let me know.)

I use a simple but powerful framework to keep our agency on track towards our long-term growth goals. It's called GOST:

Goal ➜ Objective ➜ Strategy ➜ Tactics

Here's how it works.

Start by setting your **goal**. What do you want to achieve, in general terms? What's the bigger picture? Maybe it's something like this:

'To increase our fee value'

This is a good, strong goal, but to make it measurable you also need to define your **objective**. This is what you want to achieve in more specific terms, and it needs a financial amount or a number, and a date. For example:

'An average fee value of £10,000 within 18 months'

Now you have a measurable objective to support your goal, it's time to move onto how you're going to get there. This is your general **strategy**:

'By selling more high value homes'

This is a confident and robust strategy that everyone in your office can get behind to make sure you achieve your goal and objective this year. Now you need to identify the **tactics** you will need to take you there. Here are some suggestions:

- Offer premium brochures
- Use a lifestyle photographer
- Learn how to style homes and buy some accessories
- Offer a Showcase listing so we can use it as a case study
- Don't display any low value homes on our social media
- Create content about marketing high value homes

Here's how our goal, objective, strategy and tactics look in the GOST framework:

Your 90 Day Implementation Plan

GOAL	OBJECTIVE	STRATEGY	TACTICS
WHAT		HOW	
General	Specific	General	Specific
Increase our fee value	Average fee value to be £10,000 within 18 months	Sell more high value homes	• Offer premium brochures • Use a lifestyle photographer • Learn how to style homes • Buy some appropriate accessories • List a high value home for free so we can use it as a case study • Don't list any low value homes on our Facebook page or other social media • Create content about marketing high value homes

Structuring your business goals like this makes them clearer and easier to follow. You can see exactly what you need to do to achieve them, and where you're headed. Because it's a beautifully simple plan, you can share it with your team. Have it printed big and bold to display on the wall, to keep your eye on the prize.

Download your GOST framework here: www.samashdown.co.uk/theselectiveagentbook.

Conclusion And Last Thoughts

What you need to do next

As you've been reading this book, I hope you've made a ton of notes and created specific action plans. Right now, you may be feeling a little (or a lot) overwhelmed by all the things you've learned and the activities you need to tackle. What should you do first? How do you decide what's important?

Relax. As always, I've got your back. I'm going to give you a very simple three-step checklist to make sure you start your High Value Homes Attract and Convert System in the right way, so you gain early wins and momentum for long-term success.

Step 1 – Define your ideal client using the template from www.samashdown.co.uk/theselectiveagentbook to add as much detail as possible. Share this description with your team, and ask them to each find a photo on Google of a person or couple who looks like your ideal client. Take a vote on the best fit, print it out and pin it up so you never forget who you're talking to with your marketing.

Step 2 – Create your GOST formula. Write out your goal, objective, strategy and tactics on a piece of A4 paper, and put it on the wall in your office where everyone can see it. Make sure your objective has a date in it so you can measure your success against it.

Step 3 – Get planning. Download your 90-Day Planners from www.samashdown.co.uk/theselectiveagentbook – both the blank template and the completed version. Make any changes you need to, to accommodate holidays, events, etc. Print a copy for each member of your team and share your Planners in the next team meeting. Set a start date and initial any activities according to who is going to take responsibility. Make a to-do list and share it on your team Facebook group or by email to make sure everyone knows who's going to be doing what. Revisit the Planner in each weekly meeting.

By kicking off your High Value Homes Attract and Convert System with these three steps, you'll get super focused and motivated to tackle the next three months. Today, just three steps – tomorrow, market domination!

How badly do you want it?

Throughout this book I've shown you the exact steps you need to take to attract and convert those high value homes you need to get the success you want. But I have a question for you: How bad do you want it?

It's not enough to simply try these strategies and tactics – you have to pursue them with determination and persistence. Over the last fifteen years and counting, I've learned a lot about what makes some independent agents super successful while others struggle to even get a place at the table. I've found that three special factors above all are the main determiners of success, and I'm sharing them here with you in the hope that you will embrace them wholeheartedly and take them with you on your journey to the next level.

1. Successful agents make quick decisions – no faffing, no procrastination and barely any mulling it over. They simply make decisions quickly (even big ones), and then pivot just as quickly if they need to. If a decision moves you and your business forward, it's rarely the wrong decision. And it's much better to make the wrong decision for the right reasons than to kick yourself for not taking any action in the first place and missing out on a golden opportunity.

2. Successful agents build a team of people smarter than they are – they know that they cannot do everything, and that by micromanaging the business they are strangling it. Let go, delegate, and recruit and train the best people you can almost afford. Building the best team is not cheap;

it is a significant investment but one you will be glad you made many years, and even decades from now.

3. The best agents think big – they have huge and clear visions of what they want their businesses to look like in three, five and even ten years. And they pursue those visions relentlessly. They know that what got them to where they are now won't get them to the next phase of their business growth, so they constantly evolve and develop, while always keeping an eye on the prize.

Practice these three habits: make quick decisions, build a dream team and think big, and your agency will grow and flourish beyond your wildest dreams.

When you put your faith in this system – and in yourself – amazing things happen. Lucy Joerin from Stowhill Estates in Oxfordshire told me recently that, 'It's almost scary how rapidly it has worked for us. It's like someone has put a rocket up our business backsides!'

If you'd like to know more about how we could help you install and implement the PROFIT Pyramid™ in your agency, go to http://bit.ly/bookacallwithsam and book a call with me.

Be proud of your independence

Small, local, independent estate agents are often slightly embarrassed to be seen as such, and I see them hiding behind a corporate-looking website and branded social media. But your independent status is exactly what makes a vendor choose you in the first place. Be proud of your independent standing and all that it entails: personal service, attention to detail and high-level accountability.

Vendors tend to look for a corporate agent when they need a safe option. Maybe a quick or asking-price sale is vital to them, or the market seems shaky, or they've tried an independent but it 'didn't work'. When their backs are against the wall, the higher-level properties will go to Savills, Knight Frank or Jackson Stops, and the low-to-mid properties will go to Countrywide, Your Move or a Sequence agent.

When the situation is reversed – when a homeowner feels that time is on their side so they can afford to 'test the market' or are prepared to hold out for the price they want – then they'll try a 'riskier' option. This is when they may consider an online agent or a new starter, with the added bonus of a cheap selling fee.

To attract the vendors who will value your independence, you need to spell out your differences on your website as well as in your marketing. These are the kinds of words and phrases a homeowner is looking for when they are choosing an agent for their independence:

- Truly personal service

- Help and support that is above and beyond the norm

- Going the extra mile

- Attention to detail

- Long-standing and close-knit team

- Personal accountability from the owner

- Integrated into the local community

- Family values

- Client delight, no matter what it takes

These are all elements of your service that most corporates would find hard to beat. But how do you overcome the usual list of objections that you get in market appraisals? Objections like:

- 'You're too small'

- 'You don't have the same marketing skills and reach'

- 'You don't advertise in London or nationally'

- 'You're not a well-known name out of the area'

- 'You don't have any high value properties in your portfolio'

- 'You don't have a high-street office'

Objections like these can make you feel you're on the back foot, and they can cause you to stammer and waffle. Here are some of my suggested responses. If you like them, practice them so they feel natural and flow at the right time.

'You're too small' – 'Small means less rigid, more flexible, more responsive. We can arrange viewings to suit your buyer, not our opening times.'

'You don't have the same marketing skills and reach' – 'We advertise on exactly the same property portals as all the national agents, so we are reaching the same 1 million buyers that they are.'

'You don't advertise in London or nationally' – 'I'll let you in on a little secret: agents don't advertise to find buyers; we advertise to attract sellers. As an industry, we know that print advertising doesn't sell houses, and that 98% of enquiries come from online advertising, for-sale boards, word of mouth and simply calling the buyers registered on our mailing list.'

'You're not a well-known name out of the area' – 'Buyers from out of the area don't know how many offices we have; they are simply calling the number on the board or from the online advert, which is an 0843 number – the same as every other agent on the property portals. All the buyer wants to do is book a viewing; they don't care where they are phoning.'

'You don't have any high value properties in your portfolio' – 'Our public portfolio doesn't include some very high-end properties that we are marketing discreetly for our clients. In addition, we have a "Gold Marketing Package" which will reflect the prestige nature of your property.' (Only say this if it's true!)

'You don't have a high-street office' – 'We find, in this day and age, a high-street office is a hindrance, not a benefit. By staying off the high street, we can invest in a higher level of marketing for your home, spend time on providing you with the best experience, without interruption, and make it easier for you to park when you do want to pop in to see us.'

Independent estate agents work harder

You're a cheetah, while corporate agents can be big, slow elephants. You can be responsive and react quickly to situations where speed of decision making is important. As the business owner, you are the main decision maker, which means you can make the right decisions quickly for your clients. Corporate agents often have to refer all major decisions to a head office, and responses are often slow, and communications impersonal. This is where you can win. Because in your agency, your clients receive personal service from someone who not only cares but who also has a personal accountability. Your clients' successes are your successes, directly.

Also, you are the face of your business, and that is permanent. You may have been in your town for years – how many new managers have your local corporates had in that time? Because you are part of the fabric of your town or area, you may have helped several generations of some families to move, and you hope to continue to do so for many years to come. I recently walked down Linlithgow High Street with my friend and client Paul Rolfe. It took us about twenty minutes to walk the few hundred yards to his office because so many people wanted to say hello to him, ask him questions and update him on their latest news. What a lovely position to be in, being such an integral part of his community. And I know that Paul can walk through his hometown proudly, knowing he is the best agent for those people he serves.

Tactics can be copied; personality can't

You are uniquely you, and that's what your best clients buy into. Let the corporates copy one another's tactics and strategies; they can't copy *you*. Make sure you shout loud and proud about your independence on your website with photos and information about you and your team. Open up your social media profiles to the public, so you can connect with your local community on a deeper level. That's what your clients want: someone they can trust, who has their back. Someone who they might see down the pub, or on the sidelines of an under-11 football game, or running in a charity fun run. In short, an agent who is also a friend. I would trust that kind of agent to help me move on with my life – wouldn't you?

Embrace your independence, and be proud of it. Your business, your team and your community will love you for it.

You can do it

Every business growth journey is unique, but all of you share one thing: you have the passion, determination and ability to turn your dream agency into a successful reality.

It's hard to leave you here, knowing how many unanswered questions you probably have at this part of your growth journey. As someone much wiser than me once said: it's not about the destination, it's about the journey. That's hard for me to hear when I'm scrambling up a Lakeland fell in the horizontal rain, and it will be hard for you to hear, too, when all you want is lots of lovely homes to sell and a couple of extra zeros on your bank balance. But I promise you, this journey is a gift. You'll discover things about your agency, team and clients on the way that you didn't know you didn't know. And you'll learn about yourself, too, and what you're truly capable of. One promise I'll make to you right now is that it's much more than you can dream of.

Whether you want to change everything about your business or just tweak some things, I'm here to help you. Please send me your direct mail letters and links to your blogs, and invite me to connect with you on social media. And if it's at all possible geographically, invite me to your business club. I want to share in it all and feel teacherly pride in your accomplishments. I want to see for myself how you've taken the ideas in this book and made them your own.

And keep asking – never stop. That's the only way you'll grow.

I'm going to leave the last words in this book to Seth Godin, marketing god:

'Soon is not as good as now.'

Sam

References

Chan Kim, W and Maugborne, R (2015) *Blue Ocean Strategy.* Harvard Business School Press

Deiss, R (2015) *The Invisible Selling Machine.* Digital Marketing Labs LLC

Jantsch, J (2011) *Duct Tape Marketing.* Thomas Nelson

Levinson, J. C and Gibson, S (2010) *Guerilla Social Media Marketing: 100+ Weapons to Grow Your Online Influence, Attract Customers, and Drive Profits.* Entrepreneur Press

Acknowledgements

Writing a book is hard. Really hard. But I'm lucky enough to have the best, most supportive family and friends who not only believed I could do it, but also cheered me on along the way. Here are just some of them:

Thank you, Phil – my co-director and son-in-law – for the journey you introduced me to (dragged me on) back in 2016. Without embarking on this voyage with you, this book would not be rooted in hard facts and evidence.

Thank you, Donna, who has been my steadfast writing buddy, mentor and supporter from day one.

Our wonderful AshdownJones' team – Bex, Hannah, Lois, Edward, Tilly, Maria, Laura and James – you're the best team I could ever wish for and I know the agency has been in very capable hands when I've sneaked off to write a few pages.

And my wonderful children – Paddy, Molly and Tess – for believing their mum is actually a writer.

A few people whose support means the world to me: Rita, Kathy, Penny, Sarah, Sue, Sinead and Danda.

Lastly, a big thank you to George – my faithful, feet-warming collie, who has been by my side (well, under my desk), for every single word written.

The Author

Sam Ashdown is the leading marketing expert to the UK property industry.

Her first company, www. home-truths.co.uk, was formed in 2004 to help homeowners sell more effectively. From here, www.samashdown.co.uk was established to help independent estate and letting agents to grow their businesses through smart and innovative marketing methods.

In 2017, she and her co-director launched the bespoke Lake District estate agents www.ashdownjones.co.uk, which is proving to be a leading disruptor, now selling more homes over £1 million than any other agent.

Sam often appears in the *Sunday Times, Bricks and Mortar, The Telegraph, House Beautiful* and she is the current editor for *Estate Agent Networking UK*. She has also been featured on BBC1's *Homes Under the Hammer,* and *You and Yours,* Radio 4's consumer affairs programme.

Sam is prolific on all social platforms and has a social audience of over 50,000. She travels to conferences all over the world, including *Social Media Marketing World, Content Marketing World* and *Traffic and Conversion,* all in the US. She has also travelled to Canada, the US, Nassau and Iceland, researching for a book she is writing on international real estate methods.

Sam has moved 45 times in her lifetime and now lives in Windermere, in the heart of the beautiful Lake District.

Social platforms:

- @marketingmagicforestateagents
- @samanthaashdown
- @thehometruths
- @samashdown
- www.youtube.com
  /c/SamAshdownpoweredbyFirewave